THE WONDERFUL WORLD OF WORK

THE WONDERFUL
WORLD OF

WORK

A Workbook for Asperteens

Jeanette Purkis

Illustrated by Andrew Hore

Jessica Kingsley *Publishers*
London and Philadelphia

First published in 2014
by Jessica Kingsley Publishers
73 Collier Street
London N1 9BE, UK
and
400 Market Street, Suite 400
Philadelphia, PA 19106, USA

www.jkp.com

Library of Congress Cataloging in Publication Data
Purkis, Jeanette, 1974-
  The wonderful world of work : a workbook for asperteens / Jeanette Purkis ; illustrated by Andrew Hore.
    pages cm
  Includes bibliographical references and index.
  ISBN 978-1-84905-499-7 (alk. paper)
  1. People with disabilities--Vocational guidance--Juvenile literature. 2. Youth with autism spectrum disorders--Employment--Juvenile literature. 3. Youth with autism spectrum disorders--Life skills guides--
Juvenile literature. 4. Asperger's syndrome in adolescence--Juvenile literature. I. Title.
  HV1568.5.P87 2014
  650.1--dc23
                              2013042044

British Library Cataloguing in Publication Data
A CIP catalogue record for this book is available from the British Library

ISBN 978 1 84905 499 7
eISBN 978 0 85700 923 4

Printed and bound in Great Britain by Bell & Bain Ltd, Glasgow

To Julie. Thanks for believing in me from the very start.

CONTENTS

Chapter 1

INTRODUCTION

Hi readers! Having a job is cool and has heaps of benefits which make life better both for people on the Autism spectrum and non-Auties alike. This book is all about working – it includes everything you can think of to do with the world of work.

- It aims to help get Asperteens (like you) ready to join the workforce at some point in their life. It's full of helpful hints and information to assist you in getting ready to work.

- This book will make the idea of working less scary and help you to understand just what's involved.

- *The Wonderful World of Work* aims to boost your confidence and help you to recognise all your wonderful qualities which any employer would want in an employee.

- It has heaps of cool stories about employed Auties and fun activities for you to do.

- By the time you finish the book, you should have an idea of the kind of work you may want to do and how to make it happen.

The reason I've written the book is that we Aspies tend to have a bit of trouble in getting into, and staying in, the workforce. I meet a lot of young Aspie men and women who went straight from school to disability benefit payments. I don't want that to be the only option for us when we leave school. Aspies can, and do, work and we work in all industries in many different kinds of jobs. In this book, I'll introduce you to some of my employed Aspie friends and give you some tips on finding out what you want to do for a job and how to achieve it. The book includes some fun activities for you to do which will get you thinking about how work applies to you.

ABOUT THE AUTHOR

I have Asperger's syndrome. I was diagnosed in 1994 at age 20. There were no support services for people with Asperger's when I was a child as the diagnosis was not available. I didn't like school very much because I experienced a lot of bullying, but I stayed until the end and achieved top of my year. I went to university when I was 26 and completed a Master's degree in Fine Arts, because it interested me. While I was studying, I wrote a book called *Finding a Different Kind of Normal*, which is an autobiography about my life growing up with undiagnosed Asperger's syndrome. For most of my adult life, I have had a job, but most of them were low-paid and low-skilled and weren't really suited to my level of knowledge and expertise. When I finished my degree, I landed a job in the Australian Public Service working on Government administration. I am still working for the same department some eleven years later. I love my job and feel like I am doing what I was born to do. I wish the same level of satisfaction in work to all my Aspie friends and colleagues.

WORK IS COOL!

Going to work is a great thing. I remember my first day of paid work way back in 1992 and how proud I felt to be getting on the bus and going to work like all the other early morning commuters. I was working in a fast-food restaurant but it felt special to be providing my labour in return for a wage. My housemates would tell me that I worked too hard but I didn't think such a thing was possible! Being part of something that most other people experience made me feel included and accepted into society. With my first pay cheque I bought myself a beautiful Indian doll from a shop that I loved, and I treasured this doll for many years, until it fell apart! I have been all for working ever since my first job and have never enjoyed being unemployed.

ASPIE EMPLOYEES

Some people call Asperger's syndrome a disability or a deficit. Some of them think that people on the Autism spectrum are incapable of doing all the things that other people can do, like going to mainstream school, socialising, having empathy, playing sport or working. This is not a very helpful way of treating people on the Autism spectrum and sometimes it can pull us down and make us feel inadequate. There is another way of looking at this issue and that is that we can do anything we choose to. Our Aspie thinking styles and understanding of life are actually positive attributes which others value. Qualities like honesty, dedication, loyalty and integrity are very common among people with Autism, and almost everyone, Autie or otherwise, values these qualities in a friend or in an employee. There are examples of people on the Autism spectrum doing all sorts of things that people might not expect them to be able to do. Asperger's is not necessarily a disability; it's just a different way of processing information and approaching the world. Often what makes it a disability is the attitudes of other people and of society generally. If everybody in the world had Asperger's, the world would still function. It would function in a different way to what happens now, but it would still work.

That means that we can do anything we put our minds to, within reason. We should always concentrate on our strengths, rather than our weaknesses, when thinking about our character and identity. We are changing every day and we are usually changing for the better. Your Asperger's attributes are often a positive rather than a negative, so use them!

 ## ACTIVITY
What is the best job in the world?

JOANNE – MAKING A SMALL BUSINESS WORK

Joanne is 29 and has Asperger's syndrome. She loves art and jewellery-making and is very talented. In the past, she often made necklaces and earrings for family members for special occasions. Joanne has a lot of anxiety and has found life quite difficult as a result. Joanne received a disability pension because her anxiety stopped her from being able to join the workforce. She was never very happy about this and would love to have a job like other people do, but every time she tried to work the anxiety has got the better of her and she had to quit.

About a year ago, a friend from her local Autism support group suggested she start a business, either selling her art or her jewellery. At first, Joanne didn't think that this would be possible, but her friend was insistent. Eventually, Joanne placed an advert for her jewellery on her social networking page. Her friends on social media shared the ad with their friends and before long Joanne had a large number of orders. Joanne started a webpage and now receives regular orders for her jewellery.

Instead of being anxious about her business, Joanne was excited. And she had a good head for figures so found the accounting and taxation work involved in running a business quite easy. When Joanne had worked for employers in the past she had worried all the time about making a mistake or being fired, but now that she was her own boss she felt empowered and independent. Joanne has just gone off the disability pension due to earning too much money. She is delighted and is looking into ways to grow her business further.

We Aspies often have all-consuming passions or interests. We may want to spend our whole life working with our area of interest. In some cases, these interests can translate into a job. For example, if you are passionately interested in insects, you could study to become an entomologist and then work at a university or as a lecturer or researcher. Likewise, if you are passionately interested in sports and sport statistics, you could become a sports journalist.

✎ ACTIVITY

List your passionate interest or interests and why you like them

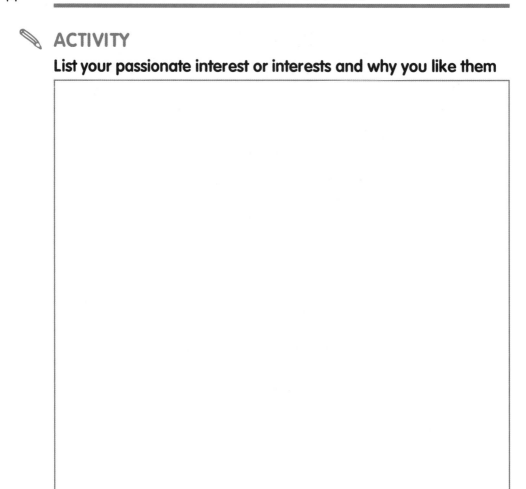

So, welcome to the wonderful world of work. We'll go on a fun and informative journey together through finding employment to wages, education and skills, interviews, applications and résumés, help for employees with Asperger's, what your rights are and what job you might want to get. By the end you'll know heaps of useful things about the wonderful world of work and should be more confident to join the workforce when the time comes for you to do so.

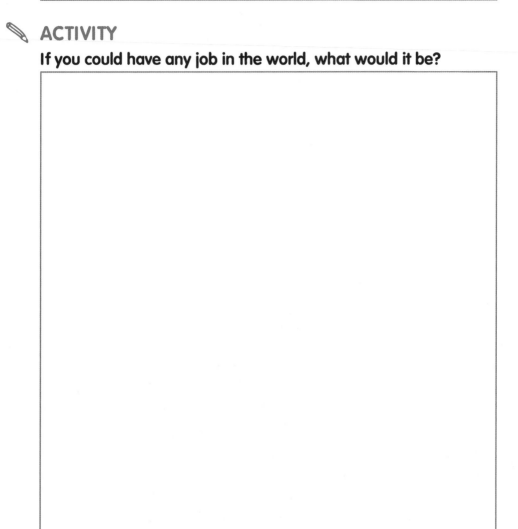

✎ ACTIVITY

If you could have any job in the world, what would it be?

Chapter 2

WHY SHOULD YOU GO TO WORK?

WAGES ARE WONDERFUL!

Not everybody works but there are a lot of reasons why going to work is a positive thing. First, there's the very obvious fact that if you go to work you will almost certainly earn more money than if you don't. Having your own money is great. If you live at home, you can buy things that you want and need, like games, gadgets, music, things related to your favourite passion, concert tickets, holidays and so on. If you live independently, it's almost essential to have a job, as rent, food, bills and transport costs, etc., add up very quickly. Every hour that you work translates into income. Working is the best way to make sure you get paid enough money to meet all your living (and spending) requirements.

It's not all about money though. Being employed improves your sense of self-worth. When you go to work, you feel good about yourself and proud of your achievement of getting a job. It's like feeling rich on the inside. Work is also a great way to pursue an interest or goal. You can work in an area related to your passion and spend your entire working life engrossed in something you love. There's a lot of Auties working in universities as professors, spending their life doing something they're fascinated with and benefiting the world with their specialist knowledge. Working also gives you a purpose – a reason to get up in the morning. It can challenge and surprise you and you can meet people who share your interests.

Another benefit of work is that you earn the respect of others and also build your self-respect when you work. Work is the ultimate key to independence. When you start working you are on that path to maturity and adulthood that all people have a right to experience. Some people think that people with disabilities or a 'label' can't work or that work is too difficult for them. That's completely wrong. Everyone should get the chance to work, whether they have a diagnosis or not. As we'll explore in this book, Auties and Aspies can be amazing employees. Go out there and prove those negative people wrong!

ACTIVITY

What would you spend your first pay cheque on if you had a job?

INDEPENDENCE IS IMPORTANT!

Going to work can also enable you to become independent and move out of home (if that's what you want). You can also afford to go out with your friends, if that's your sort of thing. Independence is great and everyone should have a chance to experience it, whether it means living by yourself or in a shared house, going to university, having a boyfriend or girlfriend or going to work. Being independent feels like nothing else in the world.

And by being independent, you're telling all those people who have told you what you can't do, that they were wrong! If you're independent you are the master (or mistress) of your own destiny. You decide how you live, where you live, how you spend your time, how you spend your money and many other good things.

SELF-WORTH IS SPECTACULAR!

Having a job is also good for your sense of personal value and self-worth. If you are unemployed, it can be very demoralising and quite depressing sitting at home all day, trying to find things to pass the time, worrying about where you will get enough money. But when you have a job, you are contributing to your own health, wealth and wellbeing and you are contributing to society (if only by paying taxes and not needing financial support from the government). You can also achieve a sense of purpose and direction when you have a job, especially a job where there are opportunities for promotion.

SOMETHING CONSTRUCTIVE TO DO

Work is a great way of filling your time. Working makes you feel as though you are doing something worthwhile and it's hard to feel bored at work, especially if you work at a busy workplace! Also, if you experience anxiety or depression, work can be a great way of distracting yourself from those negative feelings. I view my work as the ultimate distraction from my own mental health symptoms and find that I will go to work even when I feel really bad as I know that I will start to feel better as soon as I get into my tasks.

APPRECIATING YOUR FREE TIME

The funny thing about free time is that we generally do not appreciate it as much when we have an unlimited supply of it. When we go to work, especially if we are in a full-time job, we really appreciate our days off, be they on the weekend or on another day. There's nothing special about Saturday if you're at home playing computer games from Monday to

Sunday. But when you work, you find the days you have off work become particularly special and you will probably enjoy what you do on your days off much more than you did before you started work.

DON'T WANT TO WORK? WHY UNEMPLOYMENT CAN BE UNCOOL

People are unemployed for a number of reasons. Sometimes they do not have the skills needed to get a job. There may be a recession or economic problems which mean a lot of people are unemployed or they may have injured themselves or have an illness which makes it difficult or impossible to keep working. They may have lost confidence in their ability to work or they may be anxious about being in the workforce. Most people want to work, so they find being unemployed very difficult and unpleasant.

People might react negatively to you if you are unemployed. While it is wrong for people to think like this, it does happen. You will get positive feedback from peers and people you respect from having a job. If you are living with your parents and you want to move out, it will be so much harder to do so if you don't work.

If you don't have a job you will probably have very little money and may not be able to afford to do things that you want. You'll also probably be very bored. Work fills your day with productive and interesting activity most of the time. Staying at home doing nothing productive might sound like fun but it's actually quite boring for most people.

So, basically, if you go to work you have a far greater chance of having a good, independent life, being able to afford the things you want and need and having a sense of purpose and self-respect. You will have things to occupy your time and will appreciate your days off much more. You will also probably be very proud of yourself.

✎ ACTIVITY

How would having a job make you feel?

ACTIVITY

List three people you know who have interesting jobs and what they do

1.

2.

3.

Why are their jobs interesting?

Chapter 3

WHAT KIND OF WORK DO YOU WANT TO DO?

Jobs come in a huge range of types and varieties. There are dozens of industries and in each of those there are hundreds of jobs, from teachers to IT (information technology) specialists, game designers, musicians, nurses and horse trainers. Some industries have a large number of Aspies in them already, so these might be a place to start. These industries include things like acting/Hollywood, mining, transport, information and communications technology (IT) and caring professions such as nursing. In these areas, and many others, Aspies' unique skills and qualities are highly valued. In fact, some IT companies actively seek out staff who have an Autism or Asperger's diagnosis.

Here is a short list of a selection of the thousands of jobs that are out there:

- Teacher – primary school, secondary school or adult education.

- Veterinary nurse – likes looking after sick animals.

- Accountant – likes maths and calculations.

- Musician – likes expressing themselves through music.

- Visual artist – enjoys expressing themselves through visual means, like painting or sculpture.

- Disability advocate – is good at helping people with disabilities access services and participate in the world.

- Forensic scientist – likes examining scientific evidence.

- Pastry chef – enjoys making cakes and desserts for customers.

- Research analyst – is interested in finding out the answers to research questions.

- Teacher's aide – enjoys helping school children with disabilities with integration.

- Psychologist – likes to work out how people think and help them overcome emotional problems.

- Dog trainer – loves working with dogs.

- Actor – likes observing how people act and using it to play roles.

- IT technician – likes solving problems with computers.

- Academic/university lecturer – is very knowledgeable and passionate about a subject.

There's some more information about the different kinds of jobs and industries out there later in this book.

Most people have a number of different jobs over their working life. Some people find their perfect job. Others don't look for their dream job but do something which is convenient and suits their lifestyle. It pays to think big but start small when you're at the start of your working life. If you don't, you might feel a bit frustrated to start off with. This is especially true if you have to do a job which isn't matched to your skills or to what you ultimately want to do.

SHOULD YOU GET JUST ANY OLD JOB OR YOUR DREAM JOB?

Some people think that there is no point just getting any job and that they should wait until the perfect job comes up and go for that. This is not the most sensible way to approach work. Your career is a journey which starts in school and ends with retirement (perhaps to somewhere nice by the beach!). When you begin your career in your late teens or early twenties, you probably only have a few skills which employers need and little evidence of having worked before. As such, you will almost certainly want to go for low-skilled jobs which you are more likely to get. These low-skilled jobs are probably the only positions you are qualified to do at the start of your career. Some people think that low-skilled jobs are pointless, repetitive and boring. And if you see the first job you ever do as the endpoint of your career journey, you will probably not take a very positive view of your job.

A better way to view the first few jobs of your working life is to look at them as stepping stones along your career journey. You need to go across them to gain the prize of the dream job that you have wanted all along. When looking at your career it is important to take the long-term view and see it in terms of a path that lasts the length of your working life. If you go to university, you may gain a qualification to do a high-skilled or interesting job, but while you are studying you will probably need to do some kind of low-skilled job, such as working in a fast-food restaurant or supermarket. Just remember that while you do these jobs they may not be the end in themselves but that they are improving your résumé and your skills. Of course some people are quite happy to stay in a low-skilled job for their entire working life. That is fine too. The only person who can properly judge your employment choices, and the job you end up doing, is you.

DECLAN – FOLLOWING A RECIPE FOR SUCCESS

Declan is 26. Declan didn't finish school because he hated the bullying and had visual processing issues which made it difficult for him to read letters on the page. At the age of 17 he started working as a trolley collector at the local supermarket. Declan actually rather enjoyed this work as it gave him the chance to think and imagine interesting stories but he didn't feel like it utilised his creative skills.

Declan has always loved cooking and prepared the evening meal for his family on most nights since he was about ten. He is very sensitive to tastes and smells and consequently knows what flavours to put together. At 19 he started an apprenticeship as a chef in a restaurant owned by his aunt Carolyn. Declan absolutely blitzed his apprenticeship and has been working in the restaurant ever since. He doesn't really want advancement as it would involve managing people and he wouldn't feel confident at that, but he is happy doing what he loves: cooking.

Chapter 4

YOUR OWN UNIQUE SKILLS AND ABILITIES – THE BEST THING YOU HAVE!

Every person is different. We all have different personalities, different ways of thinking, different likes and dislikes and different skills and abilities. Sometimes people might try to tell you that you can't do something because you are an Aspie or that maybe you should set your sights a bit lower on something you really want to do. Sometimes these people are trying to help but often it might not seem very helpful to you. Always remember that you are a unique, amazing individual and that you have skills and abilities that other people would be very envious of. Some of the many things we Aspies tend to be very good at are:

- focusing on a topic
- understanding ideas and concepts that others find difficult to grasp
- seeing the world differently
- being loyal
- being trustworthy
- thinking differently to others
- having amazing attention to detail
- knowing a lot about subjects that interest us
- being determined
- being rational, logical and systematic

- being creative and imaginative

- being honest

- not judging other people because they are 'different'

- being sensible and responsible.

A lot of employers find these qualities very desirable in an employee. So not only do they make you a great human being, they're also an asset to you when you look for a job.

 ## ACTIVITY

Can you list three skills or abilities that you have?

> 1.
>
>
>
>
> 2.
>
>
>
>
> 3.

MAKE GRATITUDE YOUR ATTITUDE

One thing that will help you throughout your career, and life in general, is an attitude of gratitude. By that, I mean that you should approach the world, and the world of work in particular, with the idea that you have received something excellent and are incredibly lucky. The opposite to this attitude is people who look at life as if other people should do everything for them. They sometimes get described as thinking 'the world owes them a living'. This means that they think that they shouldn't have to put in any effort to make their lives better but that somebody else should do everything for them. People who think like this tend to be frequently angry and resentful at the rest of the world. Employers often find people like this very difficult to manage as they don't take responsibility for their own actions. If you adopt an attitude of gratitude you are more like to be happy and satisfied with your life. Work is not a God-given right, it is a gift. It also makes you feel better if you view life in a positive way.

You may have been told at some point in your life to 'take responsibility for yourself'. The gratitude attitude is a way of doing that. You are 'owning' your life and the decisions you make; you are not expecting somebody else to solve all your problems for you or to take the blame when something goes wrong in your life. That doesn't mean that you have to do everything for yourself starting from today though. And it's OK to ask for help from people like your parents and relatives, teachers, support people at school and doctors.

The other thing that's not a good attitude to life is called 'having a chip on your shoulder'. No, this doesn't mean that a seagull is about to swoop down and grab lunch off your back; it means you have an attitude that you are different because of your diagnosis and nobody will ever understand. People who think like this tend to be very negative and grumpy, because they think that everyone they speak to is prejudiced against them. This view doesn't just affect people with disabilities or mental illnesses; it can be found in any minority group, and even in some mainstream ones.

It is far better to look at life without this form of reverse prejudice and not have any negative expectations of the world. If somebody is nice to you, respond with friendliness, and if somebody is prejudiced against you, deal with that person but don't assume that everyone you meet will think like them. We can't know how the entire human race will act and most people are quite accepting and kind. The danger of 'having a chip on your shoulder' is that it makes you respond angrily and with resentment to everyone and so becomes a self-fulfilling prophecy. This sort of attitude is especially unwelcome in the workplace.

Chapter 5

SCHOOL, UNIVERSITY, SKILLS AND WORK

All jobs require employees to have skills. Skills are the abilities or techniques we have learned to enable us to do things. You need skills to send an email, read a book, draw a picture, even to use a TV remote! Skills needed in the workplace differ according to what the job is. A lot of jobs require IT-type skills, such as using web browsers. And a lot of jobs require employees to be able to use particular software, like Microsoft Office or Internet Explorer. Skills are the building blocks which allow everyone in the world who works to do their respective jobs.

Jobs can be put into groups according to the level and type of skills the job requires. Education – either from school or university, trade school or an apprenticeship – gives you a set of skills which you can use in the workplace. If you finish school and do some further education afterwards, like a university or trade school course, you will be more likely to get a job. And in addition to that, you can study something which will enable you to do a job that you really want to do. For example, if you're interested in mechanical workings or electrical systems you can study engineering at university and work as an engineer.

DO I HAVE TO STAY IN SCHOOL?

Put simply, statistics show that the longer you spend in education – school and after-school study – the more money you will be able to earn when you get a job. So if you want to make a good living, you should probably think about staying on at school and going to university or undertaking an apprenticeship afterwards. The opposite is also true, in that the earlier you leave school, the less likely you are to get a job at all and the jobs you are most likely to get will be low-skilled and poorly paid.

THE RESULTS FROM STAYING IN SCHOOL CAN BE COOL!

Now we all know that school can be a horrible place for a number of reasons. A lot of Asperteens leave school quite early as they feel they can't stay there any longer, and I think we can all sympathise with them. But in the long term, it's much better to stick it out and stay at school. If you absolutely have to leave, don't think of it as a permanent thing. Plan to complete your school education at a later date in an adult education setting. While there are options for completing school-level education if you drop out, it is usually better to stay in school and finish your high school qualifications and then look into what options are available for post-school study or work. If you're struggling with staying at school, try the following:

- Talking to a parent or guardian about what is going on that you're having trouble with – they might not know about the situation.

- Seeing a support person at school – a teacher's aide, learning support unit, etc. (you will usually need to get a parent or guardian to help access these services if you don't already have them).

- Talking to a friend or relative just to 'vent'.

- Reflecting on the things that make you unique and special. This might include academic ability, a high level of knowledge about a subject that most other people don't know about or drawing/ writing/acting/music/maths/science/history/language or one of the other awesome abilities that Asperteens often have!

- Looking into changing schools.

- Looking into other schooling options, such as homeschooling or the Steiner school system. Many Aspies and their parents have found homeschooling to be a very successful alternative to mainstream schooling.

ACTIVITY

List three things about staying in school that are cool!

1.

2.

3.

IF I STAY IN SCHOOL AND GET AN EDUCATION DOES THAT ALWAYS MEAN THAT I'LL GET A GREAT JOB?

Getting a good job – that is, a job that you enjoy doing and which allows you to use your skills – is a combination of many things, including the level of education you complete. Sadly there are many Aspergrown-ups who have Bachelor degrees and Master's degrees who do not have a job or who work at a level that doesn't reflect their skills and abilities. This is sometimes due to Auties lacking the confidence to join the workforce at an appropriate level and is sometimes due to them having difficulties at interviews and writing job applications. This is a sorry state of affairs and one that this book aims to help Asperteens to overcome.

But, while you may have a degree and not land a good job, you are almost guaranteed not to land a good job if you drop out of school early.

Plan your course of action, education-wise, as early as possible. If you can identify what you want to go on to do, it's a lot simpler than if you don't. But don't despair if you don't have your career path mapped out by the time you're 13! You can choose your course of action by using the checklist below:

1. What do you enjoy doing? Can it translate into an existing job or business?

2. What are you good at? Does it translate into a job or business that you are aware of?

3. What subjects do you like at school at the moment? Do you know about any jobs they might lead to if you continued studying them after school. If you don't know, is it something you can research on the Internet?

4. Do you know what kind of job you would like? If so, research what is needed to get into that industry – subjects, courses, licences or tickets required (e.g. driver's licence, health and safety pass, etc.).

5. Do you have absolutely no idea what you want to do? If so, use the list starting on page 63 to determine something you might want to do, talk to parents, teachers, friends, support workers and relatives about what they think you would enjoy and research the careers they suggest which pique your interest.

MUHAMMED – GOING BACK TO STUDY TO IMPROVE CAREER PROSPECTS

Muhammed is 20 years old and has had an Asperger's diagnosis since he was eight. While he is very smart, Muhammed found several elements of schooling difficult, particularly around concentration and his feelings that what he was studying did not relate to anything he was interested in. As a result, Muhammed left school in Year 9. He was homeschooled by his mum for around a year but he found it hard to feel motivated and the arrangement simply faded away until Muhammed was spending most of his time online, in his room, away from anybody else.

Muhammed hadn't thought much about work. He thought that he could probably live with his mum into the foreseeable future and get government disability benefits for spending money. Muhammed ended up having an argument with his mum because she wanted him to 'do something with his life' and contribute to society. As first he was angry but after a while he began to see his mum's point. Some of his uncles and cousins told him it would be good to finish his education so he could get a job too. After a while he was convinced and decided to finish school.

Muhammed is now studying for his Year 10 certificate at an adult education centre. He is enjoying the classes and likes that the other students are mostly older and mature and leave him alone to do what he wants. Muhammed is doing very well at his classes: far better than he ever did at school. He doesn't really know what he wants to do for a career, but he is finding his science classes – physics and chemistry – interesting and wonders if he might be able to have some kind of job in science.

IF YOU WANT A GREAT JOB, DO YOU NEED TO GO TO UNIVERSITY?

There are loads of after-school options which will lead to a job, not just university. There are apprenticeships, which usually last three years or so and qualify you to work in a trade-type job. Trade jobs include mechanics, plumbers, builders, carpenters, hairdressers and chefs. Some people prefer to learn skills in a practical 'hands on' way. If you are one of them, you may want to try a trade. Talk to your careers adviser or learning support unit at school if you think you would like to have a go at trades training.

There are other work skills which you can learn through a trade or 'vocational' school. These teach you more practical things which can be used in the workplace. Vocational training providers teach you practical skills to get a job. Rather than specialising in one subject, as people do at university, you can earn different certificates qualifying you to do different jobs. For example, you could gain a certificate in child care or occupational health and safety on building sites or driving a forklift or how to paint. Often, trade training is used to complement an apprenticeship. For example, you could be studying an apprenticeship in bricklaying and be sent off to gain a health and safety certificate as part of your training.

UNIVERSITY IS USEFUL!

University generally teaches you skills or knowledge centred on one area, such as medicine, nursing, teaching, accountancy, law or social work. University courses vary in length but usually run for between three and five years. There are entry requirements to university which usually involve your final marks and subjects taken for Year 12 or sixth form. Most university courses lead to a specific job (e.g. if you study law, it qualifies you to be a lawyer). However, some courses are more about expanding your knowledge and understanding of the world, like visual arts, philosophy or classics. One thing you should know about university is that the very fact that you can earn a degree often means an employer will hire you. This can be the case even if what you studied is not directly related to the work you will be doing. For example, I studied visual arts at university, but I now work in Government administration. The fact that I could stick at a course for six years, and that I had learned how to research and analyse information, meant that my employer was willing to hire me.

Sometimes, graduates will stay on at university to complete extra courses, such as an Honours year, a Graduate Diploma or a PhD. While many jobs do not require additional study, it is a requirement for others, such as clinical psychology. Doing additional study may make you a more impressive candidate in a job application process so it is worth considering.

Another thing to say about university is that it is very different from school. This goes for trade school education and apprenticeships as well. While people in school might give you a hard time for being intelligent and academically minded, at after-school institutions these things are often seen as a positive and people will admire you. The other thing about university is that you don't get a lot of help to do your work. There is not usually a learning support unit or teacher's aide. Also, lecturers will not follow up with you to see whether you have started working on an assignment or where you're up to with your work. You have to be responsible for motivating yourself and getting all your work done. This is great though and is one step on your journey to independence. And there is some help available at trade schools and universities for students with disabilities like Asperger's. When you enrol, you will get a student diary. This should have all the contact details of services you can use, including disability support services, the student union, health services, accountants, 'equity' services (like the women's room, prayer room and gay, lesbian, bisexual and transgender room) and many other cool things.

WHAT'S AN INTERNSHIP?

Some university courses, like law and medicine, have an additional year of practical study after the final year of university. This is usually called an internship. Intern doctors spend a year in a hospital, learning how to be good doctors before qualifying. Lawyers complete an intern year in a law firm, known as a 'articled clerkship'. In addition, many corporations and Government departments offer graduate programmes for people who have recently graduated from university. These years usually lead to employment with the business or department offering the programme. A graduate programme is an excellent way to commence your career and can lead to benefits throughout your career.

WILL GETTING AN EDUCATION MAKE ME RICH?

Getting a good education after high school is no guarantee of being rich but almost all the higher paid people in the world – doctors, lawyers, engineers, managers, IT consultants and so on – have studied at university. Money is not necessarily the most important thing in the world. Many people would rather have an interesting and enjoyable job than a highly paid one. Also, a lot of high-paid jobs can be very stressful as they involve a lot of responsibility, including responsibility for managing other people. In some countries, trade-type jobs, such as plumbers, builders, truck drivers or miners, are highly paid too, because they require a great deal of skill. Also, a lot of tradespeople are self-employed. Being self-employed is like running a business. Some people, including many Aspies, prefer to be self-employed than work for a manager. There are many advantages to being self-employed:

- You can set your own hours.

- You can decide which jobs to do and for whom.

- You do not need to report to a supervisor.

- If you don't want to work as part of a team, simply don't hire any staff!

- You decide how the business is run and what direction it will take.

Self-employment is definitely a career path to investigate if you have skills which you could market as a business. Your school career counsellor or an employment service provider can give you more information on self-employment. In some countries there are social welfare payment schemes that assist you to develop a business plan for self-employment, such as the *New Enterprise Incentive Scheme* in Australia.

 ACTIVITY

List three unusual, eccentric or fun courses that you would like offered in universities to help you get the skills for the world's most wacky and fun job

1.

2.

3.

Chapter 6

GETTING THE MOST OUT OF EMPLOYMENT SERVICES

Employment services are funded by governments to help unemployed people find a job. In some countries, there are services which only help people with disabilities, including Autism and Asperger's, to find work. Employment services are run by governments, 'non-profit' organisations, including charities, church or other faith groups or disability organisations. They specialise in providing employment services to help people, like you, to get a job. The sole purpose of an employment service is to help unemployed people to find work, and staff are experts in this.

Employment services help you develop a career plan, to discover what you want to do for work and explain what steps you will need to take to achieve this. Staff at these services can also help you to develop a résumé (curriculum vitae or CV) and prepare for job interviews.

Staff are usually very approachable and many of them have some training in Autism, which makes using the service a lot easier for Aspies!

Generally, you will need to be receiving some kind of welfare payment from the Government (such as disability benefits or unemployment benefits) in order to use an employment service. Using these services does not cost anything to you and, in some cases, the service may be able to pay for some of the things you need to find or start a job (such as a phone, work-boots, public transport tickets, etc.). If you cannot access a government-funded service like these, there are some private providers. These operate in much the same way as the government-funded services but you will need to pay a fee to get help from them.

AUTISM-ONLY EMPLOYMENT SERVICES

Some employment services offer help to find work exclusively to Auties and Aspies. A lot of Aspies prefer to go to a service where they know the staff have an understanding of Asperger's. Staff at Autism-only services will probably be easier to talk to and make yourself understood. That's not to say that the general services or those who cater to all people with disability are not good, but it may be worth considering using an Autism-only employment service to help you find a job, if there's one in your area. Usually these services are offered by organisations which assist people with Autism generally, such as Autism associations or societies. Please note that not all Autism organisations run an employment service. An employment service which has staff who are experts in Autism can help advocate for you in the workplace, when you get a job. They can help your managers and colleagues understand what life is like for you and how to help you succeed in the workplace. However, employment services can only talk to your colleagues and managers if you allow them to.

WHAT THEY DO AND WHAT YOU NEED TO DO

Employment services are there to support you to find a job and help you look for one and keep it. They aren't your mum though! Meaning, there are lots of things you can do to help yourself to be ready for a job. Staff at an employment service will help you with things like writing résumés and applications, practising interview techniques and building your confidence. Some things you can do to help yourself are:

- Be punctual.

- Dress neatly for interviews and work experience placements.

- Help employment service staff by answering their questions or asking them to explain something you don't understand.

- Do what the employment services staff ask you to – if that means working on your résumé, writing an application, 'cold calling' business (to see if they might want to employ you) or anything else.

You can also assist employment services to help you find a job by looking for jobs in your own time, either on the Internet or in the newspaper.

Remember that the employment service is there to help you get a job. It is working in your interests and wants you to succeed. So go for it!

✎ ACTIVITY

What things can an employment service do to help you to get a job?

What things do you think you need to do to help find a job?

Chapter 7

WORKING – WHAT IS INVOLVED AND HOW DO YOU GET A JOB?

Work is something you do either for pay or as a volunteer or as part of your own business. Most jobs out there are paid jobs for a small, medium or large business. In these jobs, the employee (you) performs some activity (work) in return for a wage (pay).

TYPES OF JOBS

The table below lists the different kinds of job type and what is involved.

	Full-time jobs	Part-time jobs	Casual jobs
Hours	Set number of hours	Set number of hours	Hours vary
Number of hours	35–40 hours per week	Less than 35 hours per week	Hours vary – no minimum
Leave	Paid holidays and sick leave	Paid holidays and sick leave	No holiday or sick leave
Pay	Same rate of pay every day	Same rate of pay every day	Extra pay ('penalty rates') for weekends, public holidays and evenings

PAID LEAVE

Full-time and part-time employees get paid holiday leave and sick leave. Holiday leave can be used for any reason. Most people use it to go on holidays or for long weekends. The rules around sick leave are a bit more strict. You can only use sick leave if you or a family member is sick. You usually need to go to the doctor and get a certificate which says that you were absent from work due to being unwell. Most doctors are very happy to provide you with a sick certificate for work – it's one of the things that doctors do most often. They usually don't write the reason you were sick on the certificate so you don't need to worry about your manager finding out if it's anything embarrassing!

SOME CASUAL OBSERVATIONS ABOUT CASUAL WORK

If you work in a casual job, you do not receive annual leave or sick leave but you generally get paid more per hour than if you work in a full-time or part-time job. You also may have access to higher rates of pay for if you work on weekends, public holidays and evenings, known as 'penalty rates'. There is no one right type of job. Some people love working in casual jobs and others prefer part-time work, especially if they have other responsibilities such as taking care of children or studying.

SUPER FACTS ABOUT SUPERVISORS

In a paid job you may have a manager who is the business owner or you might work to a supervisor. A supervisor or manager is somebody who usually gets paid more than you and is responsible for making sure you do your job correctly and quickly enough. In some businesses you will submit pieces of work, like reports or briefings, to your supervisor and he or she will approve your work to be used as part of the business. In other jobs, like at a restaurant or shop, your supervisor will oversee your work while you serve customers. It is always important to listen carefully to what your supervisor says and follow their instructions.

HOW DO YOU GO ABOUT FINDING A JOB?

There are a number of ways of finding a job. You might have a relative – such as a parent, aunt or uncle – who owns a business and wants to employ you. This is often a very good way for young people to gain their first experience of the workforce. You can also look for work online. There are a number of websites which post available jobs. These vary depending on which country you live in.

There are a lot of jobs posted online so you may wish to use the filters while you search to find jobs which you are more likely to be suited to. Filters on most of these websites include for location/city, for whether the job is full-time, casual or part-time, what sort of industry the job is in and what sort of work it is. Another good source of local jobs, and especially low-skilled and school holiday jobs, is the local newspaper. These publications usually have a 'situations vacant' section which lists jobs in your area. As we talked about earlier, you can also register with an employment service provider and they can help you find jobs.

HOW DO YOU GO FROM EAGER TO WORK TO EMPLOYED?

There is a process for applying for jobs and getting that job. These processes can be different for each industry and even each individual workplace, which can be a bit confusing, but there are a few typical processes for applying for a job, which are discussed below.

FORMAL INTERVIEW PROCESS

For a formal job application process, you usually send an application to the employer – more about how to write one of those later. You then wait to hear back – the time can vary in length from a few days to several weeks or months, usually depending on the size of the business the job is in. If the employer likes your application, you are then asked in for an interview. If they don't like your application, they will tell you that you have not been successful. Sometimes, employers won't tell you that you have been unsuccessful, they simply won't respond. In these situations it is OK to call them once or twice to ask about the progress of your application. If they tell you that you were unsuccessful, do not continue calling them. If you get an interview, afterwards the employer may call your references. We will look in more detail at how you can totally rock at job interviews and pick the best referees soon.

After that, you will hear whether you were successful or unsuccessful. Once again, if you do not hear, one or two calls to the employer to find out the outcome of the interview are appropriate. It shows that you're keen without the employer thinking you are hassling them. Later on, we'll look at how to totally blitz job interviews and get that job!

INFORMAL RECRUITMENT PROCESS

Some jobs have a very informal process for hiring employees. The kinds of jobs where this might happen are those where the manager is in your family or is somebody that your family or you know. There is sometimes a more informal process for some low-skilled jobs, too, and especially for low-skilled jobs in a small business. You might meet the boss briefly and discuss the job and what will be required of you. You might also be asked to talk about what experience you might have in employment or in doing skills related to the job. Usually you will be told quickly after the interview whether you have got the job or not.

ON-THE-JOB TRAINING LEADING TO EMPLOYMENT

There are a lot of jobs where you complete on-the-job training or an apprenticeship. The job is usually given to the apprentice on completing their study. The trick is more about securing the apprenticeship in the first place. There may be school-based apprenticeship schemes you can access through your school or you can attend a trade school which can help you start the process of getting a trade or vocational qualification. Some apprenticeships are advertised on the Internet or in newspapers.

HELP FOR EMPLOYEES WITH DISABILITY

For all these processes you can access help from disability employment providers and organisations. In some countries there are specialist disability recruitment coordinators who help people with disabilities, including Autism and Asperger's, to get a job.

SUE AND LEE – MARRIED ASPIE TEACHERS GIVING THEIR ALL FOR KIDS

Sue and Lee are married and they both have Asperger's. They are also both high-school teachers – Sue works at a specialist school for students with disabilities and Lee teaches maths at a local high school. Sue wanted to be a teacher since she was six years old. She went right through high school then university and got a graduate job teaching within months of finishing her education.

Lee has had a few different jobs. He travelled around Europe when he finished university and spent several years doing odd-jobs and short-term, casual jobs like being a short order cook and working on farms. Lee went back and got a teaching degree after he met Sue. He has now been teaching for almost ten years and sees himself continuing for the next few years.

While Sue's favourite aspect of her job is that she gets to help children who are having a hard time, Lee enjoys explaining mathematical concepts to kids. He gets a real buzz when a student who has been struggling with a maths problem suddenly grasps it and goes on to do well in the exam. Sue and Lee are very happy together and love going their separate ways each morning to different schools to do the same thing – teach.

Chapter 8

GET THAT JOB!
(INCLUDES RÉSUMÉS, INTERVIEWS AND REFEREES)

In this section we'll look at how to go about getting a job. First of all you have to decide what job you want to go for. You can go for more than one at a time and make a decision if the employers all offer you a job, just decide which one you want.

GET OUT THERE AND MARKET YOURSELF!

Going for a job is all about selling yourself to employers. Imagine that you, with all your skills and attributes, are a product that an employer needs. The best way to do this is to imagine what the employer and their business might want or need. For example, if you wanted to work in a shop selling computer hardware, you could imagine that the employer might want a worker who has a good knowledge of computers and how they work. They might also want somebody who can explain to customers how to connect peripherals to their computer and make a system work.

If you can't find a job you want online or in the newspaper, you could try 'cold calling' employers. That means that you put together a résumé and covering letter explaining your skills, and then send it to businesses that you would like to work in. You can do this via email or in person.

HOW DO YOU WRITE A RÉSUMÉ WHEN YOU'VE NEVER WORKED?

Going for your first job ever can be tricky. One of the biggest problems people face when they go for their first job is that they haven't acquired all that many work skills. Every time you apply for a job, you will need to submit a résumé. The résumé lists your educational achievements, any jobs you have done, including volunteer work, your skills and interests and referees (people who can confirm that you will be a good employee). Of course if you have never had a job, it's going to be quite hard to write a résumé which adequately explains what your skills are.

The key to writing your first résumé is to focus on your skills. Think of things you are able to do which might be useful in the workplace. Examples of this for some Aspies might be:

- using computer systems and software, especially Microsoft Office products like Word, Excel, PowerPoint and Outlook

- skills in areas which most people do not have (this could include using the Linux operating system or setting up audio-visual equipment)

- ability in writing

- ability in researching subjects

- being friendly

- being enthusiastic

- being good at maths, especially in practical situations

- starting small business ventures or websites.

A résumé will probably be different for each job you apply for. It is important to emphasise skills in each version of your résumé which relate to the job you are going for. If you apply for five jobs, you should really have five slightly different versions of your résumé, each tailored towards the job you are going for. The following résumé is for an imaginary person, James. James has worked in his parents' shoe shop since he was 15 but his main interest is in video production and cinematography. James recently completed a trade certificate in video production and is keen to find a job in the film and television industry. As part of his course, James got the chance to do work experience at a television station. He has included all of his jobs in his résumé as well as a list of his skills. James plans to send his résumé to the television stations in his area with a view to getting a job at one of them.

Example résumé, James Whitley

JAMES WHITLEY

Address 6 Legend Crescent. Uberville
Telephone 0411 111 112
Email james@awesomeaspie.com

EDUCATION

2013–14 Trade Certificate/Certificate III video production, College of Art and Design, Kuhlford

2012 School Certificate, Focus Secondary College, Kuhlford

EMPLOYMENT AND VOLUNTEER POSITIONS

2014 Work experience, Channel 10 Television. Work included observing, and assisting with, video editing for news programmes, filing, sitting in on production meetings.

2014 Busboy position, Kuhl and the Bar. Work included maintaining cleanliness in the bar, some dishwashing.

2010–2013 Retail assistant, Whitley's shoes. Work included making sales, organising the stores, cataloguing products.

SKILLS

- Video editing using Final Cut Pro suite
- Some cinematography using digital cameras (mini-DV and hard drive)
- Proficient in Microsoft Office 2010, particularly Outlook, PowerPoint, Publisher and Word, but some experience with Excel
- Hospitality – waiting, bussing, dishwashing skills
- Cash register and EFTPOS skills
- Customer service
- Good work ethic
- Friendly and diligent

INTERESTS

- Photography and cinematography
- Online gaming
- Video production
- Movies

 ## ACTIVITY

Practise writing your own résumé for the job of your choice

[Note: For a real résumé, it's best to use a table as the template and then hide the gridlines. This makes it neater and easier to read. You can also find résumé templates online.]

NAME
Address
Contact details
EDUCATION
<school>
<other courses or qualifications>
WORK EXPERIENCE
<insert if any, if not delete>
SKILLS

-
-
-
-
-
-

INTERESTS

<e.g. Blogging; creative writing; pets; making videos – try to include things related to the job you are applying for>

-
-
-

REFEREES

<Insert name> <Insert their job or relationship to you> <Insert email and telephone>

HOW DO YOU WRITE AN APPLICATION?

Most jobs require you to write a résumé and an application. The résumé is a list of your skills, interests and abilities. An application is a document which explains why you can do the job you are applying for. Applications usually involve writing to address 'selection criteria'. These are chosen by the employer and are usually attributes or skills needed to do the job. Some examples include:

- proven ability to use Microsoft Office suite of programmes

- cash register experience

- knowledge of the *Disability Discrimination Act*

- ability to use EFTPOS (electronic funds transfer at point of sale) and online banking

- a high level of written communication skills

- C-class driver's licence and clear driving record

- demonstrated ability to use Excel

- analytical research skills.

In the application, you need to describe how activities you have done demonstrate that you can do each of the skills required in the job.

A useful method of writing job applications is STAR. It stands for:

- **Situation** – What led to you doing the work? And, if possible, how does it relate to the selection criteria?

- **Task** – What were you required to do?

- **Action** – What did you do and what was the outcome?

- **Response** – How did managers or colleagues respond to what you did?

Always try to make your application as positive as possible. If you have received criticism or negative feedback from others, or if you were not good at the skills, try to think of something else you have done which demonstrates your ability to meet the selection criterion. Remember, no matter how much better it might make your application, never lie or stretch the truth. However, it is OK to use positive language about something you have done if you did it competently or well. For example, you may want to say 'I have a high level of skills in the area of editing and proofreading' rather than 'I can edit and proofread'.

When writing an application with a selection criterion of 'cash register ability', an applicant might write:

> I have a proven ability to use a cash register in a commercial setting. I have worked in my uncle's gallery since I was 15. This work meant that I used a cash register and EFTPOS machine to make sales. I am confident in using cash registers and while working at the gallery, my till always tallied up at the end of the day. My uncle asked me to work in his shop every summer during the school holidays.

Always review your application and résumé before sending them to an employer. If possible, have somebody you trust read over them and tell you if they need any changes. A parent, guardian or adult friend should be able to help you with this and will probably be very supportive and encouraging and want to help you to get the job!

INTERVIEW TECHNIQUE

If the employer likes your résumé and application, they will probably ask you to come in for an interview. You might remember that we looked at job interviews briefly in the previous chapter. An interview is an opportunity for the employer to get to know you and see how well you will fit into the workplace. A lot of Auties and Aspies do not like job interviews very much and worry that they will be unsuccessful if the employer thinks that they are odd or different.

In reality, many Aspies and Auties are very good at job interviews too. A lot of it comes down to confidence. Before the interview there are a few things you can tell yourself to get 'in the zone' and go for that job! First, you can tell yourself that, if you don't get the job, you haven't lost anything. You will simply be in the same situation. That might help you to feel less nervous. You can also think of all the things you are good at and the things that make you unique and special. Do a bit of preparation for the job, like looking up the company on the Internet and seeing their mission statement or what they do. And remember, it's natural to be nervous.

When the interview starts, shake hands with the manager and anybody else who will be interviewing you and try to be confident. Answer all the questions as well as you can, but don't worry if you make a mistake or forget something – just do your best. If you don't understand something it's OK to ask for the interviewer to explain it in more detail. Try to look in the general direction of the interviewer even if you can't look him or her in the eyes. Remember, the interviewer is trying to get to know you and find out why he or she wants to employ you, so sell yourself! Tell them about what you can do and have faith in yourself – you're wonderful! And remember that things you might think are a negative part of your character may actually be a positive. For example, if you're very keen, you might think to yourself that you're being pushy, but the interviewer might rightfully think that you are keen to work and are ready for the job.

And think of at least one question to ask when the interviewer asks if you have any questions. It doesn't have to be amazingly insightful, but a question will show that you are interested. It's OK to ask at the end how long it will be before you get the result. When it's over, shake hands with the interviewer once more, thank them for their time and leave.

WHAT TO TAKE TO INTERVIEWS (AND WHAT NOT TO TAKE)

You can take a few copies of your résumé to the interview and your application for the job. When I went for my first job way back in 1992, I took a copy of a school certificate for merit in English. The interviewer was amused by this and I felt very small and quite embarrassed. I did learn from the experience though. An employer is probably not going to be interested in seeing school merit certificates or even documentation of qualifications listed on your résumé at the interview – they just want to meet you and get an idea of what you're like. They might ask to see copies of any qualifications you have later on.

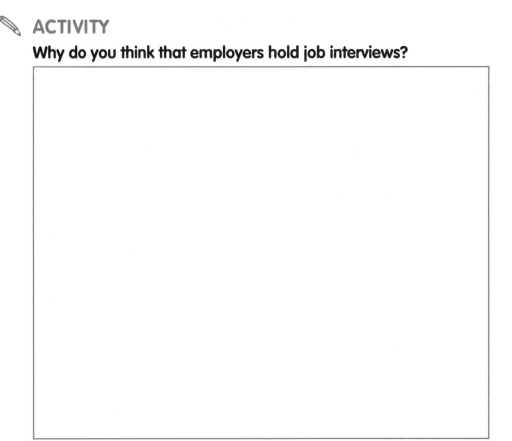

✎ ACTIVITY

Why do you think that employers hold job interviews?

WHO SHOULD YOU ASK TO BE YOUR REFEREES?

When you apply for a job, most employers will ask you to provide one or more referees. Your referees will tell the employer how good you are likely to be in the job, based on their experience of you. An ideal referee would be a former or current boss who likes your work. However, when you start out on your career journey, you may not have an employer or manager to use as a referee. You should use a trusted person who knows you well enough to tell an employer how good an employee you would be if you worked for them. You shouldn't use your parents or close relatives as referees as these people are likely to be biased and an employer would probably not take what they had to say about you very seriously. You can use a teacher, family friend, employer from a holiday job or weekend job (such as a paper round), manager or colleague from a volunteer job or an employed friend. Ideally, your referees will know you well and like or respect you. This means that they will be able to answer the employer's questions about you well and will say positive things.

When asking someone to be a referee, explain to them that you would like them to be a referee for a job. Also tell them what the job is and how much you want to do it. You can also ask them what they think they will say about you and you can discuss with them which areas you want them to focus on.

Referees can be personal – they say things about your personal qualities and attributes. These can include things like your determination, ability to focus, honesty or good character. Personal referees are usually an employed friend, a family friend or a teacher.

Another kind of referee is a professional referee. This is usually a manager or employer you have worked for. These referees can talk about your ability to perform duties related to the job, based on their experience of employing you.

You usually list your referees at the end of your résumé. You should include their name, relationship to you (e.g. 'personal reference – friend', 'former manager', 'accelerated maths programme coordinator', etc.). You should also include telephone and email contacts for them. When you ask them to be a reference for you, make sure you ask them which phone number they want you to use, as some people prefer their work number and others their mobile number.

JUSTIN – FINDING HIS PERFECT JOB!

Justin is 25 and has high-functioning Autism. He has loved buses for as long as he can remember. Justin finished school at Year 11 as he had no desire to go to university. All Justin has ever wanted to do is drive buses. To make his dream come true, he first had to get his car licence. Justin's mum helped him learn to drive and he got his licence first attempt. He needed to wait until he was 20 to go for his bus licence – that was the law. While he was waiting to turn 20, Justin researched everything he could about driving buses and went to the depot to talk to the drivers about their job. Most of the drivers liked having Justin around and he learned a lot.

Two days after his twentieth birthday, Justin applied for his bus licence. He had to put in an application to the bus depot and they would train him if he was successful. Justin wasn't quite sure who to use as a reference, but in the end decided on one of the drivers he had made friends with. This driver gave Justin a very positive reference and told the employer how keen Justin was and how he knew more about bus operations than most of the drivers! Justin's application was successful and he went on to pass his bus driving test. He has been employed at the depot for over five years now and can't think of anything he'd rather do than drive buses.

✎ ACTIVITY

What would you like your referees to say about you?

CHECKS FOR EMPLOYEES – HEALTH CHECKS, POLICE CHECKS, DRUGS TESTS, ETC.

Employers in some jobs need employees to pass tests and checks. These can include police checks, health checks or drug and alcohol tests. Usually jobs that require these things are jobs requiring a higher level of responsibility. For example, police checks (to see if employees have a criminal record) may be needed for the following jobs:

- teachers or other jobs working with children

- police officer

- prison officer

- armed forces

- government official

- nurse or doctor

- jobs working with elderly people.

These checks are to ensure that people responsible for looking after other people, or working in jobs where the public need to trust them, are good and trustworthy people. You cannot work in some of these jobs under any circumstances if you have a criminal conviction. In others, you can make a case to the employer if your criminal convictions are from a long time ago or if they were committed when you were under 18 years of age. If you haven't been convicted of anything, you do not need to worry.

HEALTH CHECKS

A lot of employers conduct medical checks on their employees prior to them starting work. While employers are not allowed to discriminate against people with disabilities and health conditions, they do need to know if you have any ongoing health problems which will stop you from doing your job. You have to be able to do the 'core requirements of the job'. If your health condition stops you from doing that, the employer may not employ you. For example, if somebody wanted to be a football referee but they were paralysed and used a wheelchair, chances are the employer would say no. Asperger's usually isn't a barrier to being able to do jobs and employers are not allowed to discriminate against you. So you shouldn't have anything to worry about from a pre-employment health check.

DRUG AND ALCOHOL TESTS

Some jobs, usually those requiring you to operate machinery or vehicles, have regular drug or alcohol tests. Jobs where this might happen include:

- airline pilot

- taxi driver

- bus or train driver

- miner

- truck driver

- courier.

These tests don't mean that you can't ever drink alcohol. It's OK to have a couple of beers the night before work in most cases. They just don't want their employees to be under the influence of substances when they are working or on call.

Employers who require police checks, medical examinations or drug and alcohol tests should tell you about it prior to it happening. In almost every case you will have nothing to worry about. And if there is something which might make you look bad to the employer, your best bet is to tell the employer about it before it shows up. Honesty is usually a highly valued quality in the workplace. And we Aspies are known for our honesty, so it's all good!

Chapter 9

VOLUNTEERING – THE GIVING KEEPS ON GIVING…TO YOU!

Volunteering means working for no pay. Volunteers often work in charity-type organisations and community services, especially in thrift shops, hospitals, homeless services and galleries and museums. It might seem odd to choose to work for no money, but there are many good reasons for doing so. If you volunteer, it shows prospective employers that you are very dedicated to working, and willing to put in a good effort. It is also a good way of gaining experience of an industry or job prior to going for a paid position. Often, managers of volunteers may offer them a paid position after they've worked there for a while. It also gives you something productive to fill your time if you are unemployed or looking for work.

In order to get some experience, you may wish to volunteer in an industry which interests you. You can include voluntary jobs on your résumé – this can actually make you look like an impressive prospect to a future employer.

Volunteering can also help you build your confidence before you apply for a paid job. Chances are, you'll be very good at your voluntary job which will help you feel ready to go for a paid position. You can also meet new friends while volunteering. Voluntary jobs have similar requirements to paid work in many respects. You may need to have an interview, although it will probably be less formal than an interview for a paid job. You may also need to undergo a police check, but do not panic because, for example, when you were 12 you shoplifted; it really is just to check that your character fits in with their organisation. Usually, workplaces with volunteers hire several of them so it can be a lovely social environment with a whole load of dedicated people with a social conscience working together.

ANDY – VOLUNTEERING HELPS HIM GET A JOB

Andy is 23 and has a diagnosis of high functioning Autism. Andy has been painting and drawing cartoons for as long as he can remember. When he finished school, Andy wasn't quite sure what to do but he enrolled in a visual art trade course. This course took a year and while he was doing it, Andy felt great. However, when the course finished, Andy had no idea what he wanted to do. He didn't feel confident to apply for a job anywhere and thought that maybe he'd have to live at home with his mum forever.

While looking at gallery websites, Andy came across a call for volunteers at a nearby gallery. While he thought that working for money would be incredibly stressful, Andy thought being a volunteer would be a lot easier. He didn't have to worry as much about getting sacked or making mistakes. After thinking about it for a couple of weeks and talking to his mum, he decided to apply.

The gallery staff were delighted to have Andy work for them. He was careful, diligent, hard-working and quiet. Andy liked working there because it gave him something constructive to do and involved a lot of tasks with artworks – hanging paintings in the gallery and installing sculptures. Andy's job involved a huge variety of tasks, from addressing envelopes, to road-testing the gallery's website to installing art. After eight months, the gallery manager offered Andy a paid part-time job as a gallery assistant. He is now studying a certificate in museum studies. Andy is making plans to move out of home when he feels ready.

Chapter 10

DIFFERENT KINDS OF JOBS

There are literally thousands of jobs you can do. Different jobs suit different people and chances are there will be one that fits your unique personality, skills and preferences perfectly. There are a number of different basic industries and within each of these a number of jobs. You can look at the list below for examples of industries, jobs within them and what kinds of qualifications you would need to work in them.

Mining – There are a range of jobs within the mining industry, from engineers to truck drivers to miners. Some jobs in mining pay very highly. You would need a degree to be an engineer but some mining jobs are relatively unskilled or require on-the-job training. If you like big machines and physical labour, mining might be a wonderful job, but can be more dangerous than other industries.

Education and training – These jobs include teachers, university lecturers, tutors, music educators, trade school instructors, integration aides, school and university administrators and school principals. Almost every job in the education and training area needs a university qualification. A lot of Aspies work in the education sector. It is a good area to work in if you have a load of knowledge about something and want to help others to understand it or if you want to help school kids obtain a good education.

Health care and social assistance – These jobs include doctors, nurses, psychologists, social workers, physiotherapists, chiropractors, drug and alcohol counsellors, mental health workers and hospital administrators. Almost all of these jobs require a university qualification. They are great jobs for people who want to help others or who are interested in biology or health sciences. They are generally very responsible jobs as they involve looking after somebody's physical or mental health.

Manufacturing – Most jobs in manufacturing, which includes process and factory work, are semi-skilled and require on the job training. There are some positions in manufacturing for engineers and managers though and these require university or trade school training. Most jobs in manufacturing are not highly paid. Advantages of working in this industry include that the work is generally quite easy and allows you time to think about other things while at work. Also you usually work set hours, which can be good if you have a lot of other commitments in your life.

Electricity, gas, water and waste services – This industry includes jobs such as electricians, electrical power line workers, workers at water desalination plants, employees at power stations, cleaners and garbage collectors. Some of the jobs are highly skilled, such as line workers, electricians and the majority of employees at power stations. These jobs are quite highly paid. Other jobs, like cleaners, are lower paid, and do not require as many qualifications. Cleaners often work very late at night or very early in the morning, which might suit an Aspie 'night-owl' very well.

Construction – Construction jobs include builders, bricklayers, plumbers, carpenters, builders' labourers and crane operators. Most employees in the construction industry have completed an apprenticeship or trade qualification. While some jobs in construction are low paid, like builders' labourers, many are quite highly paid. Advantages of working in the construction industry include that it can be very satisfying work and appeals to people who like to use their hands. A big plus of working in construction is that you get to say 'I built that!' every time you pass a completed building you worked on!

Retail trade – Retail jobs include shop assistant, store manager, packer and night filler. Many jobs in retail do not require specific qualifications. A lot of people have a job as a shop assistant as a first job after school or as a school holiday job. It is a good way of getting experience of the workplace, although generally it does not pay highly.

Hospitality – Hospitality jobs include waiter/ess, chef, kitchen hand, hotel staff, bar staff and busboy. Many hospitality jobs do not require specific qualifications, but others require an apprenticeship or trade qualification (such as chefs or hotel managers). There is often a career path in hospitality jobs, so you may be able to start as a dishwasher and work up to more responsible positions in the restaurant. A lot of hospitality jobs, especially in restaurants and bars, are very fast-paced and can be stressful. Serving customers is also a social job and can require small talk and 'chit chat'.

Transport – Transport jobs include bus, train and tram drivers, truck drivers, warehouse staff and couriers. Most of these jobs require some post-school training, which is often hands-on and undertaken on-the-job. A lot of Aspies, particularly male ones, enjoy working in transport jobs, especially bus, train and tram drivers. These jobs are highly responsible as you are in charge of a vehicle full of people and need to get them to their destination safely.

Financial and insurance services – These jobs include bank managers, call centre staff, consultants, loans officers, bank tellers, financial planners, accountants, tax agents, insurance assessors and insurance consultants. These jobs generally require some kind of university qualification or for you to undergo training after finishing school. They may appeal to people who like numbers and order, like a lot of Aspies.

Rental, hiring and real estate services – These jobs include real estate agents and property managers. They require qualifications undertaken after finishing school. Often jobs in this area are quite competitive and a large part of their salary is based on commissions – that is, the number of houses they sell determines what they get paid. Also, being totally honest when selling houses can be a drawback. However, that's no reason an Aspie can't be a real estate agent or property manager if they want to.

Public administration – These jobs include public/civil servants. The kinds of jobs that public servants do are policy specialists, people in charge of managing government programmes and services, IT specialists, government lawyers and executives. Almost all jobs in government require a university education. A lot of Aspies enjoy working in government because it is consistent and has a lot of guidelines and protocols to follow. It is usually a highly-paid industry.

Arts and recreation services – These jobs include musicians, visual artists, museum and gallery curators, events managers, actors, cinematographers, circus performers and authors. Some people in these jobs have a university qualification but it is not always necessary. A lot of Aspies work in the arts and entertainment field, particularly acting, music and writing. Jobs in this industry can be very satisfying and rewarding, although often the pay is not very good.

Aspies can be found in pretty much every single job there is. There really isn't anything that we can't do. It's just a matter of finding the right 'fit' between you and your job.

JOBS FOR ASPIES

Some jobs are more 'Aspie-friendly' than others. These include jobs where you can work alone or independently, research-based jobs (such as academic jobs at a university), technical jobs (such as engineers, IT specialists or scientists), nursing, jobs with animals (such as veterinary nursing, animal trainers, vets), special education teacher, nun or priest (for all the religious folks out there). Consider what the working environment might be like, and how 'Autie-friendly' it may be, before you decide to go for a job. That being said, there's no reason to think you won't be able to do other kinds of jobs – Aspies are everywhere in the world of work!

 ACTIVITY

After reading this list, name three jobs or industries you might be interested in working in, and why

1.
Reason:

2.
Reason:

3.
Reason:

Chapter 11

HOW TO GAIN SPECTACULAR SKILLS FOR THE WORKPLACE

As discussed previously, skills of some description are necessary for every job there is. A skill is simply something that you know how to do. Skills include the ability to use a computer, take notes, cook, drive a car, write an email, use a mobile phone, use a tablet computer, take direction from a manager and so on.

Some skills need to be learned through study. For example, a law student reads a lot of legal precedent (decisions made by judges in court). This teaches them how the law works and how to practise as a lawyer. Some skills are learned through doing. An example would be somebody whose job it is to pump petrol. And some skills are learned through a combination of studying and doing. An example would be a medical student studying to be a doctor. They learn a lot about the body and illnesses at university – called 'theory' – and then do a practical 'intern' year before they can start being a doctor. The key to using your skills to their greatest capacity is knowing how to identify them and how to determine which ones you may need to acquire.

When you start a job there may be a requirement for you to use some skills that you do not already have. That is perfectly OK. If your manager asks you to do something that you don't know how, don't be embarrassed. Simply tell him or her that you have not practised this skill before. Your manager will probably get another employee to teach you or may send you to a course where you can learn the necessary skills. Never pretend that you know how to do something that you actually don't. This can lead to difficult situations and in some jobs may even be dangerous. For example, if you say you can drive a forklift but you can't that could be very dangerous. It's always best to be up-front and honest with managers.

✎ ACTIVITY

List ten skills you have (things you can do)

1.

2.

3.

4.

5.

6.

7.

8.

9.

10.

How might these skills be useful in a work setting?

KAYLA – EDUCATING SCHOOL CHILDREN ABOUT SCIENCE

Kayla studied for a degree in zoology, specialising in Australian native marsupials. When she got to the end of her degree, she wondered if this was really what she wanted to do. Kayla remembered a visit to Scienceworld when she was a child. Scienceworld was like a museum where children went and learned about cool science-related things, like earthquakes, gravity, electricity and the human body. Kayla wondered if she would be able to get a job at Scienceworld teaching children about science.

Because she had a zoology degree, and was very enthusiastic at her interview, Scienceworld employed Kayla. Before she started, she wasn't sure about all the exhibits and was worried that she would tell the kids something that wasn't true. She called her new manager two days before she started and raised this concern. The manager told Kayla that all new staff do induction training and are taught what to say. Kayla was very relieved.

After she had done the induction training, Kayla started working on the natural history part of Scienceworld, telling children about animals, birds and the natural world. Kayla's manager was very pleased with her work and told her she'd go a long way. Now, after 18 months of working, Kayla thinks her job is exactly what she wanted to do with her life. She's happy that she studied zoology at uni because it's led her to the job. She wonders if she might get promoted one day.

WHAT ARE 'SOFT SKILLS'?

Soft skills are skills which are less obvious than most work skills, but they are just as important. Soft skills include your attitudes and behaviours. Often an employer will appreciate staff who have a good degree of soft skills. These skills include things like:

- taking direction from a supervisor

- listening

- having a positive attitude about work

- being able to cooperate with your colleagues

- being honest

- being considerate of others

- the ability to learn new things

- being enthusiastic about your job

- communicating – written and verbal

- respect for other people

- being accepting and tolerant of people who are different

- being committed to your job and your employer.

Everyone has some degree of soft skills. But even if you're not so good at some of them, you will almost certainly be good at others on the list. And soft skills, like their more practical 'cousins' in the skills world, can be learned. Chances are, if you put your mind to it, you can pick up some of them. If you're having difficulty, seek help from a trusted friend, parent or guardian. If you're already in a job, you might want to talk to your manager, supervisor or human resources area – and they'll probably be happy that you're trying to improve your skills.

SKILLS CAN CHANGE. WHAT CAN YOU DO?

Unfortunately for us Aspies, the only reliable factor in life, and especially in life at work, is that it will change. People will leave – both managers and colleagues – and new people will come along. The nature of the job will change; sometimes there will be changes in how the business is managed, the economy will change and with it the demand for what your workplace does or produces. The nature of the skills you need to do your job will change too.

The most obvious example of changes to skills is in the IT area. When I went to school we had a room full of computers. These were the only computers in the school. They did not have the Internet as it was not available for the public back in 1987. All the computers were useful for was teaching people how to type and for word processing. They were networked to a printer and it took the entire two-hour lesson to send your document to the printer and have it print. Now, the computer in your phone is more powerful than the most powerful mainframes were in the past. If you work in an industry which uses computers (and let's face it, that's most of them), the software and hardware you use will change every year or so. This change is not a bad thing as usually the changes represent improvements to the operating system, software or interface, but they are changes nonetheless. Some people are very challenged by changes in IT but they still manage to do their jobs, even if they grumble a bit.

For us Aspies, when we are in the workplace, we should expect that we will need to update our skills from time to time. It's simply a part of being in the workplace. Try not to resist it and think of it in terms of an improvement. It might make your work easier, or make you able to do your job quicker or more effectively. And your colleagues might be challenged by the change too, so you could learn the new skills quickly and offer to help your colleagues to improve at it. This could make you more popular and sought after in the workplace.

YOU MIGHT HAVE SKILLS AND NOT EVEN KNOW IT!

You may have skills that you aren't aware of. There's a particular way of thinking about skills which can help you find out which ones you have that don't immediately spring to mind.

First, think about something that you do in everyday life. It's best to think of an activity which you might use in a job. This could include using specific software products, looking after pets (for a career as a zoologist or veterinary nurse), gardening (for a horticulture or landscaping job), helping to care for elderly relatives (for aged or disability caring roles), writing a blog, using audio-visual equipment (for tech support or events jobs), shooting and editing digital video (for film production or media jobs) or keeping track of statistics on a passionate interest (for researchers, policy advisers or academics).

Now look backwards in time to before you could do that thing. What did you need to learn how to do to get to where you are now? Obviously there are skills which have more use in the workplace than others, but sometimes some of the things you can do fall within the category of 'soft skills' so it is important to look out for these too. When you have identified your skills, you can work them into your résumé so potential employers will know what you can do when you apply for a job.

Have a go at identifying your work skills in the following activity.

✎ ACTIVITY

After reading this chapter, list some work-related skills you may have discovered you have

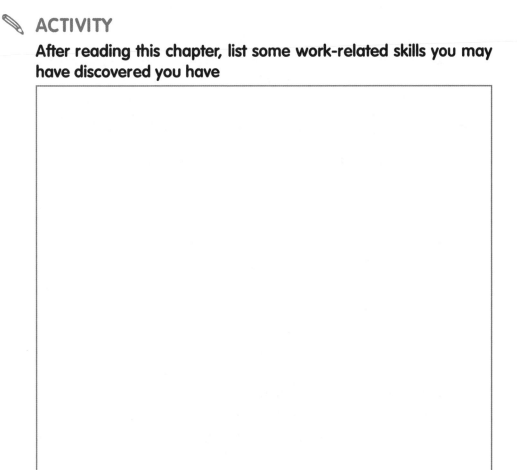

Chapter 12

JOY AND ELATION AT WORKPLACE COMMUNICATION!

In almost every job there is, employees work together with other employees to get the job done. Workplaces vary in size from a small business employing two people to a multinational corporation employing thousands of people from all over the world. All these people need to communicate with each other to get the work done. Even if you work from home as a freelance journalist you will need to communicate with the people you are selling your work to. Now sometimes we Aspies find communication a bit tricky. We don't 'get' all of what others are saying due to difficulties with reading facial expression and body language. Some of us even have trouble with understanding what the other person's tone of voice means. Basically, we usually only understand the meaning of the words the person is saying and none of the other information which non-Auties seem to be able to do instinctively. This can make workplace communication rather problematic. But that is not to say that communication is impossible or that we should give up before we start.

HOW DO YOU INTERACT WITH COLLEAGUES?

Colleagues are like your workplace family. Some of them will be like your favourite, cool uncle and you will want to spend as much time as you can with them. Others will be more like your annoying cousin who drives you mad. Regardless of how you feel about your colleagues, it is important to be polite and respectful to them and try hard to work alongside them to get the job done. Managers prefer staff members who cooperate and get along with others, so try to be that type of staff member. You may want to tell your manager or supervisor that you have difficulties understanding non-verbal communication such as facial expressions. This will help them understand why you are how you are. Knowledge is power and if you share knowledge about your experiences it will help make the workplace an easier place for you. Once you have been in your job for a while, you might want to tell some of your colleagues about your Asperger's, depending on how you feel about them. If you feel you can trust them or that they like you, it may be a good thing to tell them. This may help your colleagues to work with you in a more productive way.

There's more information about talking to managers and colleagues about Asperger's later in this book.

If a manager or colleague asks you to do something that you don't understand, just ask them to clarify what they mean. It's much better to ask for clarification than to make an assumption and possibly a mistake.

Always speak to colleagues and managers in a way that you yourself would like to be spoken to. Try not to use swear words and never use offensive language, such as racist terms. If people are talking too loudly and it's making your brain hurt, you can politely ask them to lower their voices and perhaps explain why it is upsetting you. Alternatively, you could simply excuse yourself and go somewhere a bit quieter until you've settled down. Most non-Auties do not experience sensory overload so they won't understand what it is like to have it.

Sometimes colleagues and managers will make jokes that Aspies have great difficulty understanding, like using sarcasm or dry humour. If you are confused by this, it's OK to say you don't understand it. This may provide an opportunity to talk to your managers or colleagues about Asperger's.

HOW DO YOU INTERACT WITH MANAGERS?

Every workplace has a hierarchy. This means that there are people more senior to you in the company who can ask you, and others at your level, to do jobs and tasks. There may also be people less senior, depending on your job. The manager's role is to get the people below him or her to do work. If a manager asks you to do something, you have to do it. The only exception to this is if a manager asks you to do something dangerous (that is, against Occupational Health and Safety policies and laws) or illegal.

This only happens in a very small minority of workplaces and is probably not something you will need to worry about.

As managers are people, they are all quite different. Some of them will want the job to be done in a certain way and others will want it done differently. It can take a while to get used to a new manager. It is good to be appreciated by your manager and will almost certainly make your working life easier. One thing most managers value in staff members is for them to be 'engaged'. That doesn't mean they're about to be married! It means that they are enthusiastic, or 'engaged' in their work and willing to work hard. Managers also tend to like people who are friendly and polite, those who can work with a small amount of supervision and employees who help colleagues with their work. If you try to do one or all of these things, chances are your manager will appreciate you.

Managers like to be respected by their staff. You may have a different relationship with your manager than you do with other staff at your workplace. In an office setting, some managers don't mind you going into their office while others prefer that you don't or that you knock and ask if it's OK to go in and speak to them. Some managers are more approachable than others. It may be worth asking one of your colleagues what the manager's preferences are when you start work to get an idea of how to behave around him or her. Questions you might want answered about your manager may include:

- Do they have an 'open door policy'? That is, are they happy for you to talk to them at any time or do you need an appointment?

- How do they like to be addressed – that is, by their first name or by their family name?

- Are there optional after-work socialising activities like Friday night drinks?

- Is the manager friendly and approachable or are they more 'stand-offish' and reserved?

- How long has the manager been in their position? That is, are they experienced in management or a little bit less experienced?

- How often will your manager meet with you or catch up with you about your job? This may vary in different industries, particularly in relation to how formal your meetings with your manager may be. In a bus depot, you will probably catch up with your manager at the start of the shift or during the day if there are any specific problems. In a public service workplace, you may have weekly or twice-weekly one-on-one meetings (with just you and your manager) as well as a weekly team catch-up. In a restaurant, you will be talking to your supervisor during the shift and being managed on individual tasks most of the time.

WHAT IS APPROPRIATE BEHAVIOUR IN THE WORKPLACE?

Some workplaces are different from others and the expectations of behaviour by staff differ depending on what industry you are in. However, there are some things you must never do in the workplace. These include:

- Illegal activity.

- Racist behaviour – calling somebody names or treating them differently because they are from a different nationality or ethnic background than you.

- Homophobic behaviour – calling somebody names or treating them badly because they are gay, lesbian, bisexual or transgender.

- Sexual harassment – this can include unwanted touching or attention, kissing, asking a colleague to go to bed with you, drawing attention to matters of a sexual nature about your colleague and discussing it with other staff or promising promotions or other advantages to a junior staff member if they perform sexual activities with you. These activities do not need to be sexual intercourse and can include a wide range of things. Sexual harassment is a very serious issue and employees need to be aware of what constitutes harassment.

- Angry outbursts, including yelling, breaking things and physical violence.

- Accessing pornographic or illegal websites at work.

- Sending offensive or inappropriate emails. My rule of thumb is that if you wouldn't want your mum or dad to see it, it probably shouldn't be sent to work colleagues. Offensive email content includes sexism, racism, homophobia, explicit sexual content or rude comments about colleagues or managers.

- Bullying or intimidating other staff.

These actions are never acceptable in the workplace, or even in the world outside of work. If somebody does any of them to you, alert your manager or the human resources area at your workplace and tell them what is going on. No employee deserves to be subject to any of these activities ever.

You can take the following quiz about respect in the workplace if you like. (Answers are at the end of this chapter.)

1. **A young man at your workplace uses a wheelchair to get around. One of your colleagues makes rude comments about him because of his disability. Should you:**

   A. Join in with the teasing.

   B. Tell the colleague who's making the comments that you don't like talking about people like that and leave the conversation.

   C. Yell at the person making the comments and call them names.

2. **A manager from another part of the workplace keeps sending you emails full of sexual suggestions and brushes your bottom with his hand in the lift. Should you:**

   A. Just put up with it. There's nothing you can do anyway.

   B. Punch him.

   C. Leave your job.

   D. Make a complaint to the human resources area at work.

3. **A new staff member comes to work. She is from a refugee background and is an expert in a particular area of your company's work. Do you:**

   A. Ask her 100 questions about her background because it interests you.

   B. Not give her any work because you don't think she's capable of doing it.

   C. Talk to her at lunchtime. Introduce yourself and ask her about her area of expertise.

Different workplaces have different levels of acceptable behaviour around less significant things such as what to wear to work, swearing or drinking alcohol after work. Find out what the 'unwritten policy' is as soon as you can. If you have told your manager about your Autism, you can ask him or her, or you can ask a trusted colleague. You can even ask a parent or trusted friend prior to starting the job how people in the industry you will be working in might act and what they might do in terms of social interactions. Often workplace attitudes are common knowledge even to people who don't work in the industry. For example, a parent will probably know that a truck driver doesn't need to wear a suit, that lawyers don't condone swearing in the workplace and that alcohol or drugs use isn't allowed for bus or taxi drivers.

Another thing you should be aware of is protecting the reputation of your workplace. That means that you shouldn't say rude or negative things about your workplace in public, especially on the Internet. There have been a number of cases recently where people have lost their jobs because they posted a rant about their boss on social media. My rule regarding talking about your workplace in public is to only say nice or positive things about work on any forum that the public can see, like social networks. You can whinge or vent about work to your friends and family if you like but never publish anything negative about your workplace in the public arena. Also, some jobs, like the army or the public service, make you a representative of the country. If you work in one of these areas, try to be very careful about what you say publicly about politics or the actions of the Government. You really shouldn't comment about things like the merit of your country being in a military campaign, the result you would like for an election or critical comments about government policies. However, in most jobs, it is quite OK to make comments on politics. The rule of thumb for knowing whether you need to worry about it can be whether you work for the Government. In some jobs where you are paid by the Government, like teachers or nurses, the rules are a little more relaxed as you are not considered a representative of your country. It pays to be cautious though, so bear in mind what you publish before you publish it!

ASHER – TELLING HIS MANAGER ABOUT ASPERGER'S AND GAINING RESPECT

Asher is 30. He started work as a sports journalist about 18 months ago after doing a Bachelor's degree in media and journalism. While Asher loves going to see football matches and reporting on them, he has always found the culture at the office a little challenging, as it is very 'blokey' and there is a lot of swearing and what Asher considers to be rude remarks about women made by his colleagues.

Asher has never been quite sure what to do about this. He is a very sensitive person and has a lot of respect for women. He doesn't like swearing and he also had problems with other journalists, especially the older ones, teasing him for being too 'sissy' and a 'wuss'. Asher had no idea whether they were including him or bullying him and felt very uncomfortable in the office. He would volunteer to go to any football game to report, even the local ones, just to get out of the office. He wondered several times if he should quit his job and work freelance, from home. The problem he saw with this though was that he might not get a steady income, and he didn't want to jeopardize his future just because of the blokiness at the office. When he started work, Asher didn't tell his manager or his colleagues that he had Asperger's as he was frightened that they would discriminate against him and bully him. After a while, he decided to talk to a friend about the problem. The friend suggested he tell his manager how he felt and see what happened. If his working life got worse, he could leave and go freelance, or if it got better that would be great.

Asher plucked up the courage and told his manager about his diagnosis and some concerns at work. The manager was relieved, as he had thought that Asher was going to leave his job. The manager told Asher that he was one of the best young journalists he had ever had and that he would do anything to keep him at work. Asher was surprised and delighted. They worked out a system whereby Asher could work from home three days a week. Asher was happy with it and it meant he could stay at work.

DO I HAVE TO ACT LIKE I'M AT WORK EVERYWHERE?

In most jobs, when you leave work at the end of the day you can forget about work until the next day. However, as discussed earlier, there are some jobs where you are considered a representative of your workplace or the Government, wherever and whenever you are doing your daily business. This is especially true if you wear a uniform for your job and wear it to and from work.

Jobs where this apply include:

- Army, Navy and Air-force jobs

- police jobs

- clergy jobs (priests, nuns, etc.)

- public servants and officials

- customs and prison officers

- doctors

- lawyers – solicitors and barristers.

If you decide to do one of these jobs, you will need to prove you are of good character, meaning no criminal convictions or charges. Jobs like these carry a degree of responsibility and require a level of maturity to perform well. However, many Aspies have been very successful in these roles as there are often a whole load of protocols or rules to stick to. This appeals to a lot of us. Aspies in these roles are often highly regarded due to the high level of ethics and honesty that we Aspies often have.

Answers to workplace respect quiz: B, D, C.

Chapter 13

OOH, SCARY AND EXCITING – STARTING A NEW JOB

Starting a new job can be exciting, challenging and nerve-wracking. Starting your first job ever can be those things to an even greater degree. It is important to focus on the positives when starting a new job. Instead of worrying about whether or not you will be able to do the job, it is better to think about how exciting it is to be joining the workforce, doing new things and earning money. If you are worried about starting work, you might want to ask a parent or trusted adult about the issue that is worrying you. Chances are it will be something that can be addressed and fixed.

A lot of the elements of starting work for the first time might seem scary or challenging, but there's always somebody who can help you understand what's happening and what you need to do. Try to look at your new job as the first step in the exciting adventure that is your career. Having a positive attitude can make all the difference. If you have friends your age who are working, you might want to talk to them and 'compare notes' about their job and your new job. They might even be working in a similar area to you.

Coming up in this chapter is a whole load of useful information about what it's like to start a new job.

✎ ACTIVITY

List five things you think you would need to do on your first day at a new job

1.

2.

3.

4.

5.

WHAT TO DO ON YOUR FIRST DAY

Your first day at work can be quite daunting. You probably don't know any of your colleagues yet, you might not know what you need to do and you won't know the layout of your work building. It can be really scary to start a new job, but remember, everyone else at your work has been in the same position as you at some time. It is quite likely that they will understand what you are going through and will want to help you to adjust to your new role. You might be given instructions about what to do on your first day before you start. This could include information on the physical location of your workplace, who your manager is and who to talk to when you get to work. If you do not get these instructions, you can tell someone at the workplace who you are, that you are just starting and ask who your manager is. If there is a front desk at the workplace, you can ask the receptionist. If your work is somewhere outdoors or open plan like a taxi depot or a park, simply ask one of the staff for directions and tell them you are a new employee – they should be able to point you in the right direction. You should probably leave earlier than you think you need to on your first day, especially if your workplace is located somewhere unfamiliar. You don't know how long it will take to find a parking spot and, if you are using public transport, you may not be familiar with the bus or train route which could lead to a delay. However, try not to get to work too early, say more than 15 minutes early. If you arrive too early, try to occupy your time with something enjoyable, like having a walk or buying a coffee or soft drink at a café. These things can also help you to relax a bit before you start work.

MY NEW JOB IS DESCRIBED AS 'PERMANENT'. WHAT DOES THAT MEAN?

Jobs can be grouped into permanent (also known as ongoing) jobs and temporary (also called contract or non-ongoing) jobs. The difference is that in a temporary job there is an expiration date on your employment. That means that the employer tells you how long you will be working for. After that date, you need to find another job. Permanent jobs do not have an expiration date, although you are allowed to leave and sometimes the job finishes up anyway. Sometimes if you have a temporary job you can either be asked by the manager, or apply, for the same job on a permanent basis. Many temporary employees would prefer to work in a permanent job but temporary jobs can be great for some people too, especially if they want flexible hours.

MY NEW MANAGER TOLD ME THAT I'LL BE ON PROBATION FOR SIX MONTHS. DID I DO SOMETHING WRONG?

Many jobs, especially professional-type jobs, have a period of 'probation' for new employees. If you are on probation it doesn't mean you have done anything wrong and doesn't mean you're going to prison! It's not that kind of probation. In the context of work, probation means the employer is giving you a trial period to make sure you can do your job properly and that there aren't any problems getting in the way of you being a good employee. You can usually ask your supervisor about the probation period and any concerns you have. Most employees go through a probation period when they first start a job. It is absolutely nothing to worry about and chances are you'll pass and will be able to continue working. It also works both ways: at the end of your probation you have the option of leaving if the job wasn't what you thought it would be.

TEAMWORK

Most jobs, except those where you are self-employed and working from home, involve working with people. Often employees have the same team of colleagues that they work with all the time. Often your colleagues will be at different pay levels and everyone will have different jobs to do. It's very important to work together with your colleagues. Businesses rely on employees working together to deliver results for the business.

You may find that you like some of your colleagues and not others. Sometimes some of your fellow employees will like you and others won't. All this is OK. It is important to be polite and respectful to your colleagues at all times, and particularly your manager. You don't have to be friends with all your workmates but sometimes they may ask you out for a coffee or lunch. It is OK to go with them but you can decline their offer of going out as well if you don't feel like it. If somebody does something that you think is bullying or harassment, there are acceptable ways of dealing with this that do not involve yelling or swearing at them or using physical violence. We will look at that later in this book.

MAKING FRIENDS IN THE WORKPLACE

Your work colleagues are not always your friends. Often employees do not socialise with their workmates after work hours. However, sometimes you will make friends with a colleague at work. You might spend time with them after work or on weekends and public holidays. It is OK to be friends with people at work but there are a few things you should consider about work friendships:

- Consider your work friend's level in the company. Some of your colleagues might be mistrustful or jealous of you if you are seen spending long periods of time with the boss. If you are friends with a manager, try to keep your meetings within work hours and do not discuss your friendship at length to other colleagues – they might think you're bragging or 'sucking up'.

- Try not to be too pushy about starting friendships at work. As Aspies we sometimes get very attached to a particular person, but often this person does not want to be as close to us as we do to them. If in doubt as to whether someone that you want to be friends with wants to be friends with you, ask them how they feel about being friends. Only ask once – their answer is probably not going to change.

- Office romances. Sometimes colleagues meet at work and are attracted to each other and start a sexual relationship. This can raise suspicions of other employees and lead to tension in the workplace, especially if one or both of the partners is married or in a committed relationship. My rule of thumb is to avoid workplace romances at all costs as it just adds to complexity and may make your life at work difficult.

- Some workplace friendships are strong when the two friends are working in the same area. But when one of the friends leaves to start a new job elsewhere or relocates to a different city, the friendship simply disappears. If this happens to you, try not to be too disappointed. Maybe think about staying in touch via social media. Then, you can restart the friendship at a later stage if you like.

ANXIETY IN THE WORKPLACE

As members of the Asperger's Club, we all share one thing in common in that pretty much every single one of us experiences some form of persistent anxiety. Situations of change, like starting a new job, can be extremely stressful. Often the stress is so bad it makes us want to stop doing the stressful thing. This is not a good way to approach life or anxiety. If something worthwhile is stressful, keep doing it. If you stop doing it, the stress has won. If you keep it up and stick it out and work through the anxiety, you're in charge! Also, if you do this, chances are that the anxiety will decrease significantly or disappear altogether.

Instead of avoiding the stressful but rewarding activity – in this case work – learn and use some strategies for coping with stress. These could include meditation techniques such as mindfulness or progressive muscle relaxation, talking about the anxiety to a parent, friend or counsellor, pleasant and reassuring sensory experiences, positive self-talk, breathing exercises, physical exercise or medication. Remember that anxiety about a situation doesn't hang around forever. Think of it as an experience which will pass and I guarantee you'll feel better! If stress is a big problem for you, it's a good idea to seek professional help, from a counsellor, psychologist or psychiatrist. And remember, negative things like anxiety are almost always outweighed by the positive aspects of being employed.

ACTIVITY

List some things related to working that might make you anxious

Now list some things that you can do to make you feel less anxious

WORKPLACE CULTURE – WHAT IS IT AND WHAT DO I NEED TO DO?

Workplace culture refers to the unspoken elements of being at work, such as management's attitude to the employees and vice versa, how people interact at work and how people treat their free time. If you work with a team of people, you will often be required to talk to your colleagues about non-work things, such as their kids or what they did on the weekend. A rule of thumb is to always ask them something about themselves and not just talk about your life. For example, if a colleague says 'Hi. How are you?', respond with 'Good, thanks. And how are you?' Sometimes it's hard to remember personal things about your colleagues. I always struggle when a workmate tells me on a Friday where they're going on the weekend. By Monday I've always forgotten and act surprised when they tell me about their weekend. I find that it helps to take notes – but don't let your colleagues know you are doing it. The notes prompt me to know what to ask on Monday. Small talk is a tricky but necessary part of working in a team. But remember,

Aspies who don't spend all their time chatting to colleagues about non-work matters usually impress the boss, so that's another area where Auties are awesome!

Events such as Christmas parties and farewell parties can be quite challenging. People are at work, but they're behaving as if they aren't. When people are drinking alcohol it can become very tricky indeed, especially if they have too much and get a bit loud and annoying. It is usually expected that employees will go to the Christmas party or a colleague's farewell, so it can be hard to avoid these events. You may be able to book something else at the same time, but don't do this every time there is an event or you may make yourself a little unpopular at work. While it may not always be possible to be absent from work parties, there are some things you can do to help you cope. These include:

- Leave early. This may help you to avoid dealing with drunk colleagues. It is useful to have a stash of handy excuses in case anyone asks why you're leaving. These could include 'I've got something else on', 'I'm catching up with a friend for dinner', or 'I'm not feeling so well. I might make it an early one tonight'.

- Don't worry if you find yourself not talking to anyone. Listen to others' conversations and someone might include you.

- Be clear with yourself and others on whether you are drinking alcohol or not. Set yourself a limit and stick to it. Have a glass of water between each alcoholic drink.

- Be prepared to be bored. Neurotypicals do talk about some tedious things!

- And beware of talking to neurotypicals about your passionate interests too much – they may not find them as exciting or engaging a topic as you do. Limit yourself to talking for three to five minutes about your special interest.

- If you are 'out' as an Aspie this can give you more scope to negotiate around work parties. If everyone at your workplace knows about your condition, you can probably explain if you don't want to go to work parties and why.

WHAT DO I DO WITH ALL THIS MONEY THEY'RE PAYING ME?

When you start work, you will probably be pleasantly surprised by how much money you are paid. It's great to check your bank account and find a load of extra cash that is your wages. It is a good idea to plan what to do with your cash. Sometimes you can do a simple budget by listing all your expenses and comparing them against your wages. An example is below.

IBRAHIM'S BUDGET

Salary (fortnightly): $1080 (after tax)

Expenses per fortnight:

Rent – $380

Food – $120

Transport (bus) – $50

Transport (taxi) – $60

Medication – $17 ($34 per month)

Bills – electricity, gas and water – $80

Bills – phone and Internet – $85

Savings – $150

Entertaining – $100

Subtotal – $1042

This leaves $38 after all expenses are paid

Having a budget can help you when you first start work to understand how to get the most out of your money. It is good to be able to save a bit of money for things like new computer equipment, holidays, car, new TV, and many other things which you wouldn't buy very often.

Try to keep a little money over each fortnight – that is, don't allocate it to anything, as you don't know when a large bill might come in or you unexpectedly need to go to the doctor or pay for specialist treatment. It's often a good idea to open separate bank accounts for different things, like a savings account, car account and everyday account.

If you live at home with your parents or guardians, probably the best thing you can do with your wages is save as much as you can. While it might be tempting to go out to the pub a lot or buy heaps of games, it's better to keep your money for a time for when you may need it, for example when you move out of home. Saving a rental deposit and bond is a good place to start. Money gives you power, choices and freedom.

Chapter 14

HELP FOR EMPLOYEES ON THE AUTISM SPECTRUM

Thankfully we live in a time where people with disabilities, including those of us with Autism or Asperger's, are protected from people discriminating against us. This includes in the workplace. While it's not always the case that people get treated fairly, it's much better than it was even 20 years ago.

In the past, people with Autism and Asperger's did not always get a diagnosis. In fact the Asperger's diagnosis has only been available in the English-speaking world since about the late 1980s. This means that those of us who were born before 1980 often received our diagnoses much later in life than you may have. Most of us were diagnosed as adults. While this was a negative thing for many reasons, including that there was little or no support available in school, it did mean that we did not see ourselves as needing specialist treatment. This made it easier for us to build our independence. When I left school and then home, it did not occur to me to apply for disability benefits. Instead I got a job. When I started work though, I found it very challenging and I didn't quite know how I was supposed to act. Just as I had no 'special ed' or learning support help at school, so there was no assistance in the workplace for people with Autism spectrum disorders.

Now, we're all a lot better off. Diagnoses are available for those of us on the spectrum and help is available for those of us who go to work. There are disability discrimination laws, information for managers and colleagues on Autism and Asperger's, counselling services for employees in some workplaces and occupational health and safety laws.

Even while these good things exist to make the workplace an easier place to be for people with disabilities, there is generally less help available at work than there would be at most schools. It can be a difficult transition from school or university to work, but it is well worth the effort. Mostly, adults are less judgemental of people with Autism and Asperger's than children and teenagers are at school. While if you're unlucky you might come across someone who makes life difficult for you, chances are that most adults in the workplace will be more accepting and patient than most kids would be.

TELLING PEOPLE ABOUT YOUR ASPERGER'S – TO DO OR NOT TO DO?

The decision as to whether you tell your manager or your colleagues that you have Asperger's is a very personal one. The choice is always up to you and should be made after careful consideration and thought. In my experience, I would always say you should disclose to people who need to know. For me that includes my managers at work and sometimes includes my colleagues. If you tell significant people in your life about your Autism, it allows them to understand why you may be a little different. If you don't tell them about your Autism they might make up a whole load of wrong ideas about you and why you act the way you do, which aren't true.

Also, in my opinion, Autism is nothing to be ashamed of. Therefore hiding it by not telling anyone is doing yourself a disservice. It is similar to you saying to yourself that you are ashamed of something which is not actually shameful at all – your diagnosis.

If you have told your managers that you have Autism and something difficult comes up at work that you have trouble with, it makes it that much easier for your managers to help you through it. Also, sometimes you might find something in the workplace is causing you distress, such as loud noises or fluorescent lights. If your manager knows that you have Autism it will be that much easier for him or her to make the necessary adjustments to the work environment to include you. If you choose not to tell, but circumstances arise at work due to your Autie needs, it might be the time to disclose.

Disclosing your Asperger's can help managers and colleagues to have more empathy and understanding and can make your life at work easier.

However, there may also be some issues around telling your managers or workmates about your Autism. Knowing when to tell people is a key issue. Do you let them know during the application process, at the interview, once you have started work or after you've been in the job for a little while? If you disclose your Autism during the application or interview process there is some evidence to suggest that you might be disadvantaged by it in the selection process and not get the job. Even though this is illegal in most countries and constitutes discrimination, it is often very difficult to prove it has happened. It might be worth waiting until you've got the job before you mention your diagnosis to the boss.

Some workplaces might be more accommodating of people on the spectrum than others. For example, if you want to work in the health field, teaching or other professional-type roles, it may be far more acceptable to disclose Asperger's than if you are working in mining, retail or hospitality. Ask around before you apply for a job to see what you can find out about the workplace culture of the industry where you are applying for a job. This can help to inform your decision about whether or not to disclose your Asperger's diagnosis.

You may also find that an employer or colleagues discriminate against you if you disclose your Asperger's. Some people go through their entire career without telling anyone that they have a diagnosis; others tell every single employer they ever have. In the end the decision is up to you. It requires deep thought and may be something you could discuss with a parent, counsellor, psychologist or other health professional who might be helping you.

MEGAN – ASPIE HORSE TRAINER

Megan is 26. She has loved horses since she was about eight. Megan has an incredible amount of knowledge about horses – their anatomy, how to look after them and how to interact with them. She was lucky enough to have a pony throughout her teenage years and she loved him and rode him every day. When Megan finished school she didn't know what she wanted to do. There were lots of jobs out there but none of them appealed to her.

After a while, Megan remembered visiting a horse-riding charity which helped kids with disabilities by giving them riding lessons. She had gone along to this service a few times as a young girl and it had, in part, sparked her love of horses.

Megan called the charity and offered to volunteer there by helping to look after the horses. After a couple of months, the manager offered Megan a part-time job. She didn't know whether to tell the manager that she had Asperger's and left the decision for a while as she became more experienced at the work. After a few months, Megan decided that it would be OK to disclose her Asperger's, given that the charity worked with kids with disabilities. Megan's manager and colleagues were very understanding and her manager told her that she was such a dedicated and diligent employee that it didn't matter what condition she had. Six years later, Megan is still working for the charity. She is one of the most valued and respected employees and absolutely loves her job working with horses and kids.

✎ ACTIVITY

List five reasons why it would be a good idea to tell your manager you have Asperger's

1.

2.

3.

4.

5.

List five reasons why you wouldn't want to tell your manager that you have Asperger's

1.

2.

3.

4.

5.

Chapter 15

WHAT IN THE WORLD IS WORKPLACE RELATIONS?

Workplace relations, also known as industrial relations, is a way of describing the relationship between employers (i.e. businesses, community organisations like charities and government departments) and employees (i.e. everybody that works for employers). It is a relationship which requires both employers and employees to put in their best effort. Employers could not function without employees and vice versa. In the past, and in some countries now, employers had a lot of power and employees had to work long hours for low pay with very few positive conditions such as sick leave. Over the past century, in the Western world at least, the balance has shifted to be more even and fair. However, industrial relations is in a constant state of change. Why do you need to know about this? Well, as an employee it's important to know how your workplace's policies and agreements affect you. Also, governments change industrial relations laws quite frequently and it's always good to know how this might affect your wages, conditions and the work you do.

EMPLOYERS AND EMPLOYEES – WHO DOES WHAT?

Employers are responsible for the 'bottom line'. That is to say, a business needs to ensure that it remains profitable and can stay afloat. A community service organisation or charity needs to ensure that it continues to receive enough money to stay in business and a government department needs to ensure that it is efficient and spends government funds wisely and stays within its budget. Employees exist, in a large sense, to make it possible for their employer to stay afloat. A retail employee needs to sell things to customers, a community services worker may need to write a tender or submission for government funding and a civil servant needs to stay accountable and honest and report financial matters accurately. In return, if the business stays profitable, the community services organisation viable and the government department stays within its budget, the employees will be rewarded with continued employment. If a business goes bust or a government department does not stay within budget or a community services organisation loses funding, there is potential that workers will be sacked. So, it is in the employees' best interests to do their job well.

DO BOSSES AND WORKERS BOTH BENEFIT FROM WORK?

Some people, usually very passionate political activists, have thought that employers benefit from the employment relationship with their staff while the employees are 'exploited' and have no say in how things work. This is a simplistic view of how employment works. Essentially everyone benefits from the employment relationship between employers and employees. The employer obviously benefits as they can continue to do business and make profits. But the employee also benefits, by being paid, having stable employment and, in some cases, by being given the opportunity to seek promotion if they work hard. Employees are often paid cash bonuses or receive other incentives if they work hard and deliver good results.

YOUR RIGHTS AT WORK

Work wasn't always a nice place for employees. In fact, in the Western world in the nineteenth century, most people had a pretty unpleasant time of it, working long hours and in very poor conditions for almost no money. However, employees (through their trade unions), governments and charitable organisations have worked to introduce laws which guarantee that employees have fair working conditions, including reasonable wages, decent hours and working conditions free from bullying and harassment. When you start a new job, check the contract or conditions of your employment. The employer should provide you with these. This will enable you to see what wages and working conditions you are entitled to.

Here's a fun activity to help you learn about what work was like in the past.

ACTIVITY

Research what working life was like for factory workers in 1850s London and tell a short story about what your life would be like if you were in that situation

List five reasons why work in the twenty-first century is different from work in the 1850s

1.

2.

3.

4.

5.

WHAT USE ARE UNIONS?

In some jobs and industries there are trade unions which represent the needs and interests of employees. Trade unions first gained prominence during the nineteenth century, when working conditions were very harsh for a lot of workers. They were very vocal and protested against the unpleasant situation a lot of workers experienced. These days unions have a different role as working conditions are generally a lot better now. The unions' role includes making sure workplaces are safe, supporting individual workers who may have been discriminated against at work, and bargaining with employers for new 'workplace agreements' – the documents which set out wages and conditions for employees. These cover all aspects of the working relationship, from pay rates, to the number of leave days employees can have, to allowances and bonuses which employees can receive. Some unions are more vocal than others. Usually the unions in blue-collar jobs, such as manufacturing, mining, construction and trades, are more vocal than those in professional or 'white-collar' jobs.

In most countries you do not have to join a union if you don't want to, although in some workplaces, most employees are members and there is an unwritten expectation that you join. This would usually happen in a 'blue-collar' workplace, but this doesn't happen very often. Advantages of joining a union can include that you can be assisted if anything goes wrong in the workplace, such as bullying or harassment or wrongfully losing your job. A union can also represent you in a dispute or disagreement with your manager, should one happen, although this is unusual. Unions also have a lot of deals and special offers for members and some offer income protection insurance. This insurance pays you a wage if you are off work because of an illness and injury and have run out of sick leave.

WHAT ARE MY RIGHTS AS AN EMPLOYEE?

The specific rights you have at work vary in different countries, but there are a lot of similarities between different places. Some of the rights employees have include the following:

- Be paid for their work. Rates of pay are different in different jobs, but there is a 'minimum wage'. You must be paid the minimum wage or more.

- Be allowed to work free from discrimination or harassment. This includes discrimination on the grounds of disability, like Autism or Asperger's.

- Be protected from unfair dismissal.

- The right to 'freedom of association' – that is, the right to join, or not to join, a trade union and to be free from being pressured in this decision from either the trade union or your employer.

Chapter 16

TROUBLE AT WORK! WHAT DO I DO?

Some Aspies experience difficulties in the workplace. In fact, neurotypicals also experience difficulties from time to time. These difficulties can usually be overcome and employees can get back to a productive and enjoyable experience at their job. Now we'll look at things to be aware of and find out some solutions which may help improve the situation:

- Communication problems – not knowing what to say to managers or colleagues and/or how to say it.

- More communication problems – not understanding what other people mean by their words or actions.

- Not understanding the unwritten 'rules' of the workplace.

- Physical environment problems – such as noise, fluorescent lights, etc.

- Small talk with colleagues.

- Issues about whether or not to disclose that you have Asperger's syndrome to colleagues and managers.

- Workplace bullying.

- Difficulties with dealing with change (such as the need to acquire new skills or move to a different part of the workplace).

- Difficulties with becoming distracted and not focusing on work tasks or becoming too focused on a particular task.

If you are aware of these issues, you can probably do something about working to address them.

106   THE WONDERFUL WORLD OF WORK

- There are many books out there about how people with Asperger's can improve their communication skills.

- You can also seek help from a counsellor, psychologist, parent or friend if you're having trouble with non-verbal communication or hidden meanings.

- You can ask your manager for 'reasonable adjustments' to help you do your job. These could include replacing fluorescent lights with incandescent ones, reducing noise levels, wearing headphones, etc. Note: you need to disclose that you have Asperger's to access these kinds of adjustments to the work environment.

- If you cannot structure your time or have difficulties remembering tasks, write everything down! If prioritising tasks is difficult for you, you can initially ask your manager to help you.

- If you have trouble with being distracted by noises or other things, you could try listening to music on an iPod or MP3 player.

There is usually a solution to most workplace problems and issues. If you have a good relationship with your parents, an adult friend or a counsellor, psychologist or other health worker, you can discuss the problem with them and they might be able to help you to come up with a solution.

ACTIVITY

Can you think of a problem you might come across in the workplace?

What would you do to overcome that problem?

While it might seem daunting to put yourself in a position where these things might happen and have you thinking 'Do I really want to join the workforce?', all these issues can be overcome with the right support and expertise. Also, there's no guarantee that any of these things will happen to you; they're just a list of possible difficulties that some Aspie employees may face. There's a reasonable chance that you will only experience one of two of them if any and they are all fixable. The world of work is a far more Autism-friendly zone in the present day and things continue to improve.

BULLYING – IT'S NEVER OK, BUT IT STILL HAPPENS

Chances are you've experienced bullying at school. It happens to pretty much everyone at some time or another and it happens a lot to kids with Asperger's. It's a sad fact of life that schools, parents and kids are working to overcome but it is still far too common.

I often think of children as being less sophisticated adults. So while a child will say exactly what they think and give little thought to whether or not it might cause offence, an adult will keep those blatantly insulting and hurtful things to themselves. Even though the adult won't come straight out and say or do anything insulting, they might still be thinking similar thoughts to the high-school bully. The hurtful thoughts might come out in another way, such as excluding the person they don't like from activities or conversations, or trying to undermine them in the workplace. They might gossip behind the person's back or interfere in their friendships or relationships. These things are bullying too and they are just as unacceptable as when it happens in the schoolyard.

Bullying like this can happen in the workplace. And the more obvious and overt bullying like that which might happen in school can also happen in the workplace. That's not to say that it will, but it is important to be aware of the potential for issues with bullying. The good thing is that bullying is now illegal and is considered by pretty much everyone to be wrong in the workplace. There are people and services you can talk to if bullying in the workplace is happening to you.

The steps you can take are:

1. If you are able to, raise the issue with the person who is treating you badly. They may be unaware and, most importantly, it is considered the most appropriate first step.

2. If you cannot raise the issue with the bully, or you have and it has not achieved anything, raise the issue with your manager. If the bully is your manager, raise the issue with their manager.

3. If this doesn't work, and your workplace has a human resources department, raise the issue with them. They will almost certainly have procedures for dealing with workplace bullying.

4. If this doesn't resolve the issue and you are a member of the trade union, raise the issue with your union representative.

5. If this doesn't work, you may like to consider moving to a different area in the workplace, finding another job or taking the matter to court.

It is hoped that you will never have to go down this path, but the information is there in order to prepare you should you need to address a matter of workplace bullying.

PERFORMANCE – WHAT IS IT AND HOW DOES IT WORK?

Performance means how well you do your job. Your job might consist of a number of elements. For example, a taxi driver needs to be able to drive a car safely and within the road rules. He or she also needs to be civil to passengers, and also to make cash transactions. They also need to be able to read a map or use a GPS (global positioning system) machine. If the taxi driver does all of these things well, they will be a high performer. If they do some things well but not others, for example they are an excellent driver and can find their way but they are rude to customers, their performance will be more patchy. Some people are very high performers and others underperform.

Managers tend to be very interested in their employees' performance because it affects how well the business does in terms of sales or production or any other element of what keeps them in business. When you start a new job, your performance will generally not be as good as when you have been in the job for a while. Managers know about this and usually make allowances for it. They might send you off to do a course or training which relates to a part of your job, or they might ask a more experienced employee in the firm to help you out, just for the first few weeks.

Your performance can also change depending on other things going on in your life. When I bought my first home, my manager told me that my performance had slipped as I was quite preoccupied with the arrangements for buying my house. Shortly after I moved in, my performance went back to its previous level.

Sometimes your Asperger's will mean that you are more stressed about something than other employees might be. This was definitely the case for me when I bought my house. If you have disclosed your Asperger's to your manager and you have a performance-related issue because you are stressed, it would be helpful to explain to the manager about Asperger's and how it can increase anxiety. Never assume that your manager, colleagues or any other person knows what it means to have Asperger's, even if you have told them about the diagnosis. Not everyone knows what it means. Explaining your situation to others can help other Aspies as it increases knowledge of the condition among ordinary people.

You will get the most out of your job if you are a high performer. High-performing employees from all industries and jobs often share similar skills and qualities. They are often:

- committed to doing a good job

- willing to accept comments and constructive criticism from managers or colleagues

- good at paying attention to detail

- honest and trustworthy

- willing to put in an extra effort when needed, like staying back after work on occasion

- accepting and respectful of colleagues and managers, including those from other cultural backgrounds, who have disabilities, who are gay, lesbian, bisexual or transgender, or who have different religious views

- able to listen to instructions from managers.

Aspie employees often have a number of these qualities and managers frequently regard Aspie employees highly for their attention to detail, work ethic, honesty and commitment to their job.

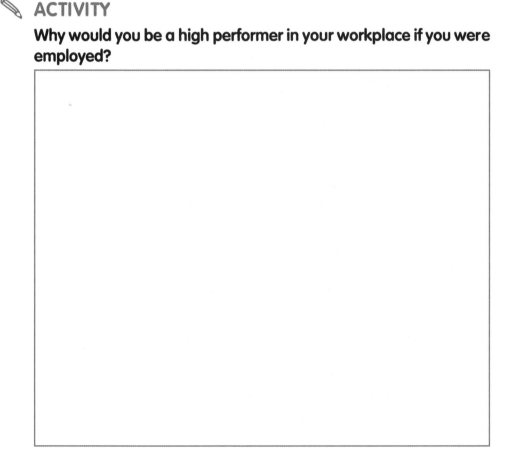

✎ ACTIVITY

Why would you be a high performer in your workplace if you were employed?

Chapter 17

BEING BRILLIANT IN YOUR OWN BUSINESS!

If you don't want to work for a manager and you have a product or an idea that other people might want, you can go into business. Businesses range in size from a 'sole trader' where an individual person sells products or services, to a multinational corporation. Usually businesses start small and work upwards. Advantages of having your own business include that you are your own boss, you can be creative, you make all of the decisions and you can be as ambitious as you like with real prospects of doing well for yourself.

There are a couple of disadvantages of having a business though. These include that it can be risky to have a business, especially if the economy is in a downturn. Business owners can find themselves worrying about the future of their business. Also, if you employ staff, there can be a lot of rules and requirements – i.e. paperwork!

However, a great plus about owning a business is that you can do it at the same time as having another job, or studying, or raising kids. A small-scale business – for example, somebody who sells home-made jewellery – can start off as a means to supplement income or 'test the waters' before making a firm commitment to the business.

Some businesses which you might be interested in could include:

- proof-reading or editing services

- video production

- music production

- portrait or pet photography

- computer maintenance, trouble-shooting or tutorials

- gardening

- dog walking

- painting, drawing or sculpting

- talking about Autism (for example to schools, police, workplaces, etc.)

- website design and maintenance.

 ## ACTIVITY

If you had your own business, what would you sell, produce or provide?

There might be something else you want to do as a business. If it's a service or product that people need, you might be in a great position to capitalise and make a successful business. A lot of very innovative and creative people have Asperger's, so don't feel constrained from getting out there with your brilliant business ideas!

LI – MUSICAL GENIUS WHO MAKES THE MOST OF HIS GIFTS

Li is 38 years old and was diagnosed with Asperger's when he was 31. Since he was a small boy, Li has known that he was special. He can pick up and play any musical instrument. He plays music with amazing amounts of expression and feeling with perfect pitch. Li has always known that the only career path for him involves music.

Li runs a business whereby he arranges and produces music for all sorts of people who are good at one instrument, or are good singers, but who don't have Li's incredible talents for putting it all together. Li has a long list of satisfied customers. He also plays as a sessional musician for a number of organisations and individuals. He has played at weddings, in church, at birthdays and for film and television.

Li has played music professionally since he was a young teenager. To Li, being a professional musician did not even need consideration – he always knew that was what he wanted to do. Li uses the focus and determination that come with his Asperger's to do a better job in his business. He realises that his gift for music is also an advantage of being an Aspie, so he doesn't mind very much that he has the diagnosis.

Li gets the chance to make his own music too. The only drawback of Li's choice of work is that he doesn't always get a reliable income as some months there is more work than others. Li knows how to save and budget though, so this isn't all that bad.

Chapter 18

GETTING READY TO GO FOR IT…

I hope you have learned a lot from reading this workbook. And I hope it's given you a better understanding of what work is like, why working is great and what you need to do to get ready to start work. It is hoped that by now you have some ideas of what you might want to do when you start on your career journey.

I hope you enjoyed reading about all my employed Aspie friends and that they've given you a bit more confidence to get out there and go for a job.

Some final points you might want to think about:

- A job is the passport to a future. If you work, it gives you a bunch of good things, like an income, self-confidence, something productive to do with your time and independence.

- It's almost always better to be employed than unemployed. Even if you get a job which isn't perfect, it can lead to bigger and better things, work-wise.

- Independence is awesome! Get up, stand up and look up into your future as an independent human being. Everybody has the right to an independent life, especially us Aspies.

- I know it's hard, but try to stay at school as long as you can. If you need to leave early, it's not the end of the world as you can pick it up later on in adult education. But education is the key to getting the job you want.

- Aspies are extremely good at a load of things that are valued by employers in the workplace. Aspies generally have great attention to detail, are passionate about a subject, logical and systematic, accepting and tolerant, honest, loyal and trustworthy and see the world from a different point of view.

- Aspies can, and do, achieve anything. I can pretty much guarantee that Aspies are out there right now, doing the full range of jobs. There are Aspie engineers, cooks, teachers, electricians, horse trainers, artists, music producers, authors, actors, waitresses, nurses, academics, mums, childcare workers, train drivers, flight attendants, pilots, scientists, public servants, florists, psychiatrists, sailors, integration aides and so on. We are truly everywhere! You have every right, ability and chance to join the ranks of employed Aspies when you're ready.

- Think positively. It can make all the difference.

- Remember that the first job you ever do is very unlikely to be the one you are doing when you retire. Your career is a lifelong journey.

THE AUTHOR'S STORY – A MANY AND VARIED CAREER WITH A HAPPY ENDING

Jeanette is 38 and was diagnosed with Asperger's when she was 20. Jeanette started out working at a fast-food restaurant. Although she didn't enjoy it very much, she stayed for two years and was promoted to junior manager. However, Jeanette had some negative things happen in her life and left the workforce for many years. She was determined to rejoin the workforce though and went to university in order to gain a qualification.

Jeanette studied visual arts at university and had numerous exhibitions. This gave her some experience of the business world. She was very poor and lived in a public housing estate, so she decided to work towards getting a full-time job so she could move somewhere nicer.

Jeanette was very anxious about working as she had been unemployed for a long time. She started out volunteering. This helped her to gain confidence. Then she started up a small business editing videos for other students at university. This helped Jeanette by giving her some extra income, but the main benefit from it was the increased confidence Jeanette felt. Then she got a job presenting talks to schools about Asperger's plus a job collecting for charity. At this point her confidence had vastly improved and she applied for a full-time job in the Australian Public Service. Jeanette's application was successful and she joined the department a few months later. It involved a move to Canberra, which was stressful, but Jeanette took it in her stride as she knew her job was an overwhelmingly positive thing.

Jeanette has been working for the same department since 2007. She has been promoted twice and loves her work. Jeanette has been told by colleagues that she was born to be a public servant. In 2013, Jeanette received an award from the CEO of her department. The award was for excellence in making the department a better place for employees with disabilities and promoting inclusion in the workplace. Jeanette is so grateful that she has a good job which she enjoys. She hopes that everyone will achieve similar things in their careers, and especially readers of this book. :)

Final activity – well done!

ACTIVITY

What is your ultimate job?

What are the things you need to do to move towards getting it?

Asperteens: you are amazing. You can do it! Go out there and get that job!

GLOSSARY

Aspie – Someone diagnosed with Asperger's syndrome.

Autie – Somebody diagnosed with an Autism spectrum condition.

Autism and **Asperger's syndrome** – These terms are used to describe Autism spectrum conditions. They are used interchangeably and without distinction. The author is of the opinion that while somebody may have received a diagnosis of 'Asperger's syndrome' their condition is just as accurately described by the umbrella term 'Autism'.

Being 'out' – Telling people about your Autism or Asperger's diagnosis/ disclosure.

'Bottom line' – In a business, the level of profitability, i.e. how much money, or profit, a business makes.

CV ('curriculum vitae'), also known as a résumé – a list of your achievements, skills and qualifications that you give to an employer when applying for a job so that they know whether or not you can do the job.

Employment service – An organisation which assists unemployed people to find work. These include specialist employment services for people with disabilities including Autism.

Human resources – The area of a company that deals with all things staff-related, like pay, recruiting new staff, working conditions, sick leave and dealing with poor work performance. Not all businesses will have a human resources department and they are usually found in larger organisations.

Induction training – Training new employees undertake to learn about their new workplace and what is expected of them by their employer.

Neurotypical – Somebody who does not have a diagnosis of an Autism spectrum conditions.

Vocational – Meaning to do with work. Vocational training is training related to doing a job.

FURTHER READING

Edmonds, G. and Beardon, L. (eds) (2008) *Asperger Syndrome and Employment.* London: Jessica Kingsley Publishers.

Purkis, J. (2006) *Finding a Different Kind of Normal.* London: Jessica Kingsley Publishers.

Santomauro, J. (ed.) (2012) *Autism All-Stars.* London: Jessica Kingsley Publishers.

WEBSITES

Aspritech (ICT company which actively seeks out staff with Autism): *www.aspiritech.org*

Australian Autism and Asperger Network Inc.: *www.aaanetwork.com.au*

Autism Aspergers Network Magazine: *www.aanmag.com.au*

Australian Government Department of Employment: *www.employment.gov.au*

Autism Star: *www.Autism-star.com*

CNN: *www.cnn.com*

Job Access: *www.jobaccess.gov.au*

United Kingdom Department for Education: *www.education.gov.uk*

United Kingdom Department for Work and Pensions: *www.dwp.gov.uk*

INDEX